BLACK DOG OPERA LIBRARY

Cavalleria Rusticana
I Pagliacci

BLACK DOG OPERA LIBRARY

Cavalleria Rusticana

PIETRO MASCAGNI

I Pagliacci

RUGGIERO LEONCAVALLO

TEXT BY DAVID FOIL

**BLACK DOG
& LEVENTHAL
PUBLISHERS**
NEW YORK

Published by
Black Dog & Leventhal Publishers, Inc.
151 West 19th Street
New York, NY 10011

Distributed by
Workman Publishing Company
708 Broadway
New York, NY 10003

Designed by Alleycat Design, Inc.

Series editor: Jessica MacMurray

Photo Research: Diana Gongora

Book manufactured in Hong Kong

ISBN: 1-57912-018-0

h g f e d c b a

FOREWORD

Cavalleria Rusticana and *I Pagliacci* are intense, brutal and concise operas, written to reflect the Italian movement, *verismo:* "truthism". At the time of their conception, Italian culture was enraptured by bold brutality, raw emotion and violence through art—these two exemplify this trend. Forever tied together, *Cavalleria* and *Pagliacci* reveal, and in fact celebrate, the most ruthless and animal of human emotions through stories that take the audience back to a highly-stylized nineteenth century Italy.

Explore the pages of this book: learn about the origins of the operas, the lives of the composers, and the world of opera singers and conductors. Listen to the complete opera on the two CD's included in the inside front and back covers of this book, while following along with the complete libretto. You will find both an English and an Italian version, complete with annotations by the author.

Enjoy this book and enjoy the music.

ABOUT THE AUTHOR

David Foil is the author of the six-volume Black Dog Music Library and the first four volumes of the Black Dog Opera Library. A native of Louisiana, he has written extensively about music, theater and film, both as a critic for newspapers in the South and as an annotator for a wide range of classical recordings for the Angel/EMI classics, Columbia and Sony Classical labels. He lives in New York City.

RUGGIERO LEONCAVALLO (1858-1919)

Cavalleria Rusticano

I Pagliacc

PIETRO MASCAGNI (1863-1945)

They are the bad seeds of opera, blunt and shocking twin melodramas about common people driven by the most pitiful of human weaknesses, virtually possessed with unbridled sex and longing, consigned to their fates in a hale of murderous violence. And the public has never been able to get enough of them. *Cavalleria Rusticana* and *I Pagliacci* have been enormously popular for a little over a century, since each enjoyed a sensational premiere in Italy in the early 1890s. Today, we think of them as inseparable mini-masterpieces, ideally matched in their stories, in their profusion of melody and in their blistering intensity. Both

operas ignited a curious little revolution in opera, one that was over virtually as it began. And they were written when their composers were relatively young men, soaring to international acclaim and wealth, only to be cursed with never again being able to equal such success.

Cavalleria Rusticana came first, premiering May 17, 1890 in Rome and igniting such a frenzy in Italian audiences that it is generally recognized as the first successful opera in the vivid style known as verismo , which means realism. Its composer, Pietro Mascagni (1863-1945), wrote the opera with the idea that he might enter it in a prestigious competition for one-act operas sponsored by the publishing house Sonzogno. The source was a short story of the same title, which translates as the ironic "Rustic Chivalry," by the Italian writer Giovanni Verga. (Mascagni later claimed that, when the time came, his wife entered the work in the competition without his knowing, while he was still wondering if, instead, he should enter the fourth act of his opera *Guglielmo Ratcliff.*) Mascagni won the Sonzogno competition. The premiere of *Cavalleria Rusticana* began inauspiciously: the Teatro Costanzi in Rome was only half-filled. But the audience greeted the opera with hysterical ovations. Word of its success spread instantly and, within a year, it had been performed around the world. There were places in Italy where audiences demanded, as they cheered a performance, that the entire opera be repeated. Such euphoria led to the composer being hailed immediately as the long-sought successor to Giuseppe Verdi, the aging master of modern Italian opera.

Mascagni was born in Livorno on December 7, 1863, just as Verdi was coming into his own as the most popular, successful and powerful Italian composer the world had known since Rossini's active years. But Mascagni's roots were humble—his father was a baker who expected his son to take up the family trade—and it was only with the aid of an uncle that he won the argument. His uncle's help allowed him to attend the Milan Conservatory, where he studied with the brilliant composer Amilcare Ponchielli *(La Gioconda)*. Mascagni had little interest in the discipline of study, however, and he was thrown out of the conservatory in 1884. He made a living by conducting operetta and teaching, though he continued to compose. The unimaginable success of *Cavalleria Rusticana* after its premiere transformed Mascagni's career, if not his very real but limited gifts as a composer. Mascagni was, in many ways, a victim of the 20th century, where his music would be judged superfluous and his choices and allegiances would prove personally disastrous, right up to his death in 1945. Though his career after the turn of the 20th century was intermittently successful and gratifying—many of his later operas are thrilling entertainments, badly underrated— he was haunted and ultimately frustrated by the long shadows cast on that amazing night in Rome in 1890.

Pagliacci emerged two years later, as a direct result of its success of *Cavalleria Rusticana*. Its composer, Ruggiero Leoncavallo (1857-1919), had so far failed to implement his pretentious dreams of creating a monumental Italian operatic form that echoed Richard Wagner's visionary music-dramas. He seems to have been at least as gifted as librettist as he was a composer. From all indications, when he set out to write *Pagliacci,* Leoncavallo was looking simply to create something that would establish him as a force to reckon with in the Italian opera world. Taking note of the success Mascagni was enjoying, he concocted a little thriller of his own. In this case, there was no literary pedigree; Leoncavallo wrote his own original libretto, basing it on a case he remembered from the courtroom of his father, a police magistrate in Naples. *Pagliacci* premiered on May 21, 1892 in Milan's Teatro del Verme—Arturo Toscanini was the

RUGGIERO
LEONCAVALLO,
1904

conductor—instantly generating the same kind of wild excitement that propelled *Cavalleria Rusticana* to international success within a year.

Ruggiero Leoncavallo was born in Naples on April 23, 1857, into a family that encouraged his musical inclinations. He entered the city's conservatory when he was only nine years old, beginning a decade of training that seemed to prepare him for great things. From the beginning, Leoncavallo had an uncommon literary gift that pointed him in the direction of opera. But his efforts in 1878 to stage his first opera, *Tommaso Chatterton,* were not successful, and he began wandering Europe as a café pianist. In Paris, he discovered the music of Wagner, which had a decisive influence on him, prompting him to envision a multi-opera Italian Renaissance epic not unlike the German's *Ring* cycle. Leoncavallo probably imagined himself laughing all the way to the bank on the commercial success of *Pagliacci,* as he pursued his real goal of becoming the new visionary of Italian music. He did become a rich man from *Pagliacci,* but his later serious efforts were blighted, in one way or another. Even Leoncavallo's successes were stung by failure. His 1897 setting of *La Bohème,* for instance, is a skillful, richly melodic opera, quite different from the one by Puccini (whom the livid Leoncavallo believed stole the idea from him); its only serious flaw is that it simply is not a work of genius, as Puccini's is. By 1905, Leoncavallo had turned to operetta, which he composed and conducted prolifically, notably among Italian audiences in the U.S. He was haunted and embittered by his failed efforts to duplicate the triumph of *Pagliacci,* even though—for a brief, shining moment—that stunning success made him the new Verdi, the new Mascagni, the new hope.

Neither Mascagni nor Leoncavallo would know this kind of success again, though it was not for lack of trying. (In American popular music, this kind of success came to be called the "one-trick pony.") Mascagni was the luckier of the two, though even his more ambitious later operas would ultimately fail to hold the stage, even in Italy. Leoncavallo died in 1919, his promise delivering little more than a few indifferent full-length operas and a series of undistinguished commercial operettas. Aside from *Pagliacci,* he is probably best known for the radiantly beautiful song "Mattinata," which he wrote (text as well as music) for a recording he made with Enrico Caruso in 1904. Mascagni lived long enough to become a genuine has-been, extravagantly embracing Mussolini's Fascist regime in the hope that it might help him restore the luster of his fading glory. He died just as World War II ended, an invalid largely forgotten and reduced to living with his wife in two rooms of a Roman hotel. His last taste of the spotlight came in 1940 when he conducted (with grindingly slow tempos) a series of performances and a landmark recording of *Cavalleria Rusticana,* on the 50th anniversary of its premiere.

If both composers had a legitimate shot at being recognized as Verdi's successor, those hopes were dashed, almost cruelly, by the astonishing rise in the 1890s of another composer well-known to both men, Giacomo Puccini. Mascagni and Puccini had been friends since their student days in Milan, even living together at one point; stories from their penniless student days are believed to have inspired the young artists' escapades depicted in Puccini's *La Bohème.* In later years, their contrasting fortunes strained their friendship. Leoncavallo and Puccini were the same age, and Puccini hired (and subsequently fired)

Leoncavallo as the librettist for his first successful opera Manon Lescaut. Leoncavallo would soon develop a consuming hatred for Puccini, whom he contended stole the idea of *La Bohème* from him. The potentially explosive verismo revolution in Italian opera that began with Mascagni and Leoncavallo all but came to an end with their success. In truth, neither composer wished to be viewed strictly as a *verismo* composer. They wanted what Puccini discovered— a transcendent new style, informed by the vivid intensity of *verismo,* but also echoing the power and glory of Verdi's most effective operas. By the turn of the 20th century, Puccini's success had begun to make his one-time friends look like a pair of also-rans.

Verismo is a term that is broadly applied to Italian opera beginning with Mascagni, Leoncavallo and Puccini. Like the term *bel canto,* it is often misunderstood. *Verismo* was a literary style first, inspired by the controversial impact of the great French realist Emile Zola. Giovanni Verga countered Zola's work with a new kind of Italian literature about contemporary life that avoided any effort at prettifying the world or the people inhabiting it. Part of the attraction of verismo was its regional flavor, as well as its grim, almost cruel fascination with squalid lives ruled by the animal instinct. Audiences were shocked (and fascinated) with this unblinking candor and vividness. If conservatives were disgusted, enlightened bourgeois readers and audiences were intrigued, as they had begun to chafe at the artifice of a great deal of late 19th-century culture. By the time Cavalleria Rusticana reached the stage, Verga was a greatly admired author and the Italian audience knew his work very well.

On the operatic stage, such a gritty melodrama had rarely been seen anywhere. There had been realistic portrayals of contemporary life in all its anguish, without the trappings of myth or history—Verdi's *La Traviata* was, in many

ways, a forerunner of verismo opera. So was the French composer Georges Bizet's *Carmen*. But both were also great love stories, in which—despite tragic endings—love carried the day. The plots of *Cavalleria Rusticana* and *Pagliacci* involve the kind of people who, in our culture, populate tabloid-TV talk shows. *Cavalleria Rusticana* tells of the fate of a Sicilian village stud, Turiddu, who has ruined the life of one local girl (Santuzza) and is in the process of breaking up the marriage of another (Lola). The cuckolded husband (Alfio) calls him out—with the vile gesture of biting him on the ear—and brutally stabs him to death. In Pagliacci, we meet a troup of commedia dell'arte players arriving in a Calabrian village. They are led by the psychotically jealous and abusive Canio. He fears his girlfriend Nedda is unfaithful to him, which she is, with Silvio (a somewhat

PLACIDO DOMINGO AS TURIDDU AND
PAULINE TINSLEY AS SANTUZZA IN
CAVALLERIA RUSTICANA

more caring version of Turiddu). The catalyst in the drama is Tonio, deformed and none too bright; he is himself obsessed with Nedda, though she is disgusted by him. Courtesy of Tonio, Canio learns of Nedda's infidelity and is destroyed. Later he has loses his grip on reality onstage, going berserk and slaughtering Nedda and Silvio before a horrified audience.

Cavalleria Rusticana and *Pagliacci* are perfect examples of the verismo style in opera. For, as beautiful and memorably melodic as the music may be, it tells a harsh and brutal story in both works. There is no apology for the awful dramas that unfold or attempt to moralize about their characters. Nobody really "learns" anything about himself or herself; these simple, peasant-like people simply do what their instincts tell them, and live (or die) with the consequences. Few other operas, even from the same period, achieve the same lean honesty quite so rigorously. But the elements of documentary-like candor, vivid cruelty, raw carnality and fierce emotion that power verismo opera would outlast the fad of the style itself. Puccini wrote brilliant *verismo* operas in *La Bohème* and, much later, his one-act thriller *Il Tabarro.* But his triumph was in successfully applying those elements in more traditional operatic settings—Napoleonic Rome in *Tosca,* Japan in *Madama Butterfly,* the American Wild West in *La Fanciulla del West.*

Mascagni tried to do the same in his later operas, including *Iris* (set in Japan), *Il Piccolo Marat* (set in revolutionary France) and *Isabeau* (a mythic drama). Leoncavallo, in particular, wanted to write operas that ranged far from the hot, dusty Italian countryside. He failed utterly to realize his Wagner-like trilogy about the Italian Renaissance entitled *Crepusculum;* the first opera *I Medici* was almost laughed off the stage, and he never wrote its companion works about *Savanarola* and *Cesare Borgia.* Not even the German Kaiser could force his court to get excited about the opera Leoncavallo wrote for him in 1904, Der

Roland von Berlin. In fact, Leoncavallo's only palpable operatic successes in the wake of *Pagliacci* were *Zazà*, an opera about gypsies, and his own, inevitably overshadowed version of *La Bohème*. Both operas are *verismo* in spirit, if not in literal style. The same can be said of the operas of such contemporary Italian composers as Alfredo Catalani *(La Wally, Loreley)*; Francesco Cilea *(Adriana Lecouvreur, L'Arlesiana)*; Umberto Giordano *(Andrea Chénier, Fedora)*; Italo Montemezzi *(L'Amore dei tre re, La Nave)* and Riccardo Zandonai *(Francesca da Rimini, Conchita, Giulietta e Romeo)*. But a cosmopolitan sound and style were blended here with the vigorous directness of Italian opera. The influence of Wagner's richly orchestral and schematic writing can be heard and felt in the work of all these composers, as well as later developments of Richard Strauss and even Claude Debussy.

ROSALIND SUTHERLAND AND DENIS O'NEILL IN A WELSH NATIONAL PRODUCTION OF PAGLIACCI, 1996

If *verismo* made new and stringent demands on composer, librettist and audience member, they were nothing compared to what was now being asked of the singer. A pundit once noted that *verismo* helped invent the flip side of *bel canto* singing—a style irreverently dubbed *can belto*. If *bel canto* style asked a singer for a graceful, perfectly contrived sense of line and a beautifully modeled vocal sound, *verismo* seemed to demand the opposite. Driven by base emotions, with nothing to lose, Mascagni and Leoncavallo's characters express themselves stridently, crudely, belligerently, often in ways suggesting that a pretty vocal line and a consistently beautiful sound were beside the point. The vocal writing is tightly woven into the orchestral fabric, and most conductors have not been able to resist driving the volume as relentlessly as the drama. Singers quickly learned that stamina and sheer lung power were necessary to prevail. Fortunately for *Cavalleria Rusticana* and *Pagliacci,* their success coincided with the rise of a singer who would transform the art of the Italian tenor and the role of the singer in contemporary culture—Enrico Caruso.

Caruso made his professional debut in 1895, and Turiddu in *Cavalleria Rusticana* was one of the first roles he learned and performed. Canio in *Pagliacci* became, perhaps, his signature role. Other tenors, of course, enjoyed great success with these roles, including the consummately stylish Fernando de Lucia, a generation older than Caruso and the leading Italian tenor of his day. De Lucia was a favorite of Mascagni's (he later sang in the premieres of the composers *L'Amico Fritz* and *Silvana),* and he made priceless acoustical recordings of Canio's great solos from *Pagliacci,* a glimpse into the style of singing heard at the time of these operas' premieres. In those recordings, it is easy to hear that De Lucia holds back nothing in terms of passion, thought he never fails to deliver singing that is, aesthetically, a thing of beauty in itself. Caruso's sound was dramatically different—bigger, shinier, with a hint of baritonal power, virtually an assertion of *machismo* in singing. His recordings of the tenor arias from *Cavalleria Rusticana* and *Pagliacci* are thrilling, and they are probably a pale imitation of what he delivered onstage. He raised the stakes in performance, suggesting a new style in which the singer seemed to go for broke with every performance. Like de Lucia and despite their differences, though, Caruso was apparently a remarkably consistent and pleasing performer. But those who sang with him and followed him had to contend with the standard he set.

The new style transformed singing, though not everyone tried to out-sing Caruso or each other. The palpable feeling for the vibrant characters of verismo opera led to a more credible level of theatrical performance in opera, reflected in the singing in various ways. When Mascagni recorded *Cavalleria Rusticana* in 1940, the Turiddu was the great lyric tenor Beniamino Gigli (also a memorable Canio), his honeyed voice still in superb condition, offering a fascinating counterpoint to Caruso's more muscular interpretation. Lyric voices have taken their measure of these roles—Luciano Pavarotti as Canio, for instance—and found success in them.

The leading roles in both *Cavalleria Rusticana* and *Pagliacci* have been transformed over the years by the ways singers approach them. In *Pagliacci,* Tonio has a showcase in the splendid Prologue that opens the opera; baritones have all but institutionalized the addition of a stunning high A-flat (an exceptionally high note for a baritone, two steps below a tenor's high C) at the end of the Prologue, a note Leoncavallo did not write. Even more striking is what happens in the opera's final moment. When Canio murders Nedda and Silvio, the brutally ironic line "La commedia e finita" is spoken...invariably, now, by Canio himself. The line was originally Tonio's, and it is unquestionably one of the great moments in Italian opera. But it makes scant dramatic sense for Canio, who has literally lost his mind, to be lucid enough to utter this adroit observation. Just try telling that to a tenor who is singing the role and wants the last word.

In both operas, the quest for dramatic edge has led to liberties being taken with tempos and musical values. Sometimes a vocal line cannot contain the drama of the moment. At the end of their confrontation in *Cavalleria Rusticana,* Turiddu literally shoves Santuzza aside to go after Lola. Santuzza is shattered, at the end of her rope, and in her rage hurls a Sicilian curse at him—"A te la mala pasqua!" (An evil Easter to you!). How could such a line (or the exchange that directly leads to it) be simply sung? Some singers go a little crazy; there is a recording of a live performance from La Scala in 1963 (the centenary of Mascagni's birth) in which it sounds as if Franco Corelli and Giulietta Simionato are literally going to kill each other. On the accompanying recording here, listen to Corelli and Lucine Amara. Their fury is palpable, and Amara literally wails the famous curse. Just as tellingly, the next thing she utters—an insult addressed to Turiddu, "spergiuro" (betrayer)—is sung with an almost Wagnerian intensity, over a boiling orchestra crescendo, complete with cymbal crashes. When he conducted *Cavalleria Rusticana* at the Metropolitan Opera in 1970, Leonard

Bernstein resolved to rid the performance of any "traditional" additions to the score. But when he heard Mascagni's own recording, in which seems to condone the taking of liberties with the printed score, Bernstein gave up. Such alterations have become part of the sound of both operas.

In emphasizing the hard edge of *verismo* opera, we must not underestimate the sheer beauty of the music Mascagni and Leoncavallo wrote. The writing often lacks sophistication but just as frequently has it in spades. The pastoral calm of the prelude to *Cavalleria Rusticana* is brilliantly interrupted by Turridu's offstage serenade to Lola—a bewitching clue to the drama that is about to unfold. The opera's most famous passage, the beautiful orchestral Intermezzo, breaks the unbearable tension with a brief, sad meditation on what has happened and what is inevitable. In Pagliacci, could Canio's despair be more perfectly expressed than in the recitative-like aria "Vesti la giubba," crowned by those agonizing, masochistic cries of "Ridi, pagliaccio" (Laugh, clown!). Nedda's *ballatella* is just as inspired, a fantasy of emotional freedom that is both touching and ominous.

As the accompanying recording demonstrates with eloquent power, the genius of Mascagni and Leoncavallo in *Cavalleria Rusticana* and *Pagliacci* is not simply one of brute force. They savor these little dramas completely, through lean and compelling narratives, with characters that are indelibly etched. When a great cast rises to the occasion, as is the case here, the effect is electrifying and...well, *real.*

The Story
of Cavalleria Rusticana

In the distance, the voice of the swaggering Turiddu breaks the quiet of an Easter morning, singing a *Siciliana* in which he serenades his lover Lola. The villagers prepare to go to church, bubbling with excitement about the pleasant weather and the beauty of the spring morning. There is plenty of sexual tension: even as they are about to attend Mass, the men of the village sing of their admiration and longing for the women, as the women rejoice in the sensuous atmosphere of nature in bloom. The gloomy figure of Santuzza enters, going to the wineshop run by Mamma Lucia, Turiddu's mother. Mamma Lucia tells the girl her son has gone earlier to a nearby village to take delivery of some wine. But Santuzza tells her this is a lie; Turiddu was in the village the previous night. Mamma Lucia tries to invite her in, but Santuzza refuses, for she is an outcast. The teamster Alfio enters the square, full of pride in his work and passion for his beautiful young wife Lola. When she asks him, Alfio tells Mamma Lucia that he had indeed seen Turiddu the night before, as Santuzza said—in fact,

CATANIA, SICILY—THOUGHT TO BE PART OF THE INSPIRATION FOR CAVALLERIA RUSTICANA

Alfio had seen him near his own house—leaving the old woman shocked and concerned. Alfio scoffs at idea of going to church, but the spectacle of the Easter service begins to dominate the square with the singing of the *Regina coeli,* which is heard within the church and echoed in the square by the distraught Santuzza and arriving churchgoers. As the crowd disappears into the church, Santuzza explains to Mamma Lucia why she had given the old woman a sign to show no

TURRIDU INVITES THE CROWD TO
MAMMA LUCIA's—CAVALLERIA
RUSTICANA

surprise at Alfio's news. She and Turiddu had been in love, she reveals, but he had betrayed her with Lola. While Turiddu was away serving in the military, Lola tired of waiting for him and married Alfio instead. On his return, Turiddu took up with Santuzza again, making love to her, but once again betraying her with Lola. Alfio was frequently away, and his affair with Lola was easy to continue. Seduced, abandoned and reviled, Santuzza has no one to turn to. Mamma Lucia agrees to pray for her when Turiddu returns suddenly. He treats Santuzza coolly, and she attacks him for returning to Lola. He tries to lie about it but sees that Santuzza will not accept his answer. He opens up to her, telling her that he fears for his life if Alfio finds outs. Santuzza, still in love with him, is moved to forgive and protect him. But Lola turns up, ironically, singing an alluring song that shows just how vain and shallow she really is. She sees Santuzza with Turiddu, and she sneers at them. When Turiddu turns to follow her into the church, Santuzza finally understands how faithless Turiddu is. The two fight angrily, though the pitiful girl is reduced to begging Turiddu to take her back. He is repelled by her neediness and the way she literally clings to him. Angrily, he shoves her to the ground and goes to the church to find Lola. Shattered and without hope, Santuzza hurls an awful Sicilian curse at him— "A te la mala pasqua, spergiuro!" (An evil Easter to you, betrayer!). Alfio returns to the square and Santuzza, in her hysteria, tells him the whole story of Lola and Turiddu. As Turiddu predicted, Alfio is filled with a rage that encompasses a threat to kill his wife's lover. Santuzza runs out, horrified at the events she has set in motion. When the mass ends, everyone leaves the church, including the illicit lovers. Turiddu is so exhilirated to be with Lola again that he invites everyone to Mamma Lucia's for a glass of wine. He sings a drinking song as the glasses are filled. Alfio has joined the crowd, but he refuses Turiddu's wine. With a bite on the ear, he challenges Turiddu to satisfaction for the betrayal, and Turiddu agrees to settle the issue. As everyone else flees, Turiddu is left alone and he tells Mamma Lucia two things—that he has drunk too much and must go away, and that if he fails to return she should be a good mother to Santuzza. Mamma Lucia gives him her blessing. She cries as he leaves, but Santuzza returns to embrace her. The women of the village come running back into the square, and one of them is screaming that Turiddu has been killed.

The Story
of I Pagliacci

PROLOGUE

Wearing his clown's motley and makeup, the character Tonio steps through the curtains to address the audience. He announces that the author has opted for an old-fashioned prologue to the evening's entertainment. Only this time, it will not reassure the audience that the show's *commedia dell'arte* characters are only play-acting. This story, Tonio insists, is a true one. The passions are real and deadly. And with that understood, he says, let the show begin.

ACT I

The setting is rural Sicily, in Calabria, near the village of Montalto, on afternoon of August 15, the Feast of the Assumption, probably around 1870. A troupe of players enters the square in a covered wagon. The villagers are drawn by the promise of a show, though there appears to be trouble behind the scenes. Canio and Beppe quarrel until Canio steps forward to drum up a crowd for a show at 11 p.m. that evening. Tonio enters with Nedda, and the tension between Tonio and Canio is so obvious that the villagers wonder if they are both in love with Nedda. Canio tells the crowd not to confuse reality and the play, for his character Pagliaccio might be generous about his lover's faithlessness, while he, Canio, would not. The crowd scatters to go to Vespers. Nedda is disturbed by Canio's expression of jealousy but, at that moment, a flock of birds streaks across the sky, and she yearns for their freedom. Tonio, who is deformed and simpleminded, watches her in rapture. He pours out his passion to Nedda, who is so disgusted she grabs Beppe's whip and lashes Tonio across the face. He runs away, screaming in pain and threatening revenge. In fact, Nedda does have another lover, the handsome villager Silvio, who comes to her after making sure Canio is away. Nedda tells Silvio about Tonio's declaration and her response. Silvio begs Nedda to stay behind with him when the troupe leaves the next day. But the confused actress refuses, and Silvio lashes out at her. The little tiff ends with her confessing her love for Silvio when Tonio returns to eavesdrop. The lovers are in each other's arms when Tonio drags Canio in to witness the scene. Silvio tells Nedda to meet him at midnight and slips away before Tonio and Canio can catch him. Canio turns his rage on Nedda, threatening her with his

stiletto to reveal her lover's name. Beppe rushes in and disarms him, reminding him that they must prepare for the performance. Left alone, as his psychotic rage curdles into self-pity, Canio first decides he cannot do the performance. Then, as he mechanically applies his makeup and dons his costume, he tells himself the show must go on. The clown must laugh, even as his heart is breaking.

ACT II

The villagers gather for the evening's performance. The curtain rises on a typical *commedia dell'arte* farce. The simpleminded servant Taddeo (played by Tonio) makes a pass at his appalled mistress Columbina (Nedda) while his master Pagliaccio (Canio) is away. Columbina's actual lover Arlecchino (Beppe) arrives on the scene with a plot

JAMES KING AS CANIO AND EMILY RAWLINS AS NEDDA, 1980

to poison Pagliaccio. He is almost caught when the furious husband returns home sooner than expected. Pagliaccio accuses Columbina of having a lover. At this point, Canio begins to lose his grip on reality; he can no longer differentiate between the patented situation of the play and the anguish in his own life. But he pulls himself together as Columbina tells Pagliaccio it was, in fact, Taddeo. Taddeo shouts a confirmation from the wings, which makes the audience laugh. Enraged, Canio turns on the audience, then Nedda, demanding the name of the lover. The audience is taken with the fervor of the performance, though Nedda realizes Canio is slipping over the edge. In character, she begs Taddeo to confirm that Arlecchino had been with her, but she refuses to name a lover. Canio explodes in rage, demanding the name, as it becomes clear to the crowd that they are no longer watching a play. He grabs a knife and stabs Nedda. She dies calling Silvio's name, and when the young man rushes to the stage, Canio stabs him, as well. The crowd pours onto the stage and disarms the murdering clown, as he ironically announces, "La commedia è finita!" (The play is over).

Cavalleria Rusticana

PIETRO MASCAGNI 1863-1919

Santuzza...Victoria De Los Angeles
Turiddu..Franco Corelli
Alfio...Mario Sereni
Lola...Adriana Lazzarini
Mamma Lucia...Corinna Vozza

Conducted by Gabriele Santini
Orchestra e Coro del Teatro dell'Opera di Roma
Chorus Master: Gianni Lazzari

I Pagliacci

RUGGIERO LEONCAVALLO 1858-1919

Canio..Franco Corelli
Nedda...Lucine Amara
Tonio..Tito Gobbi
Beppe...Mario Spina
Silvio...Mario Zanasi
Peasant I...Franco Piva
Peasant II..Angelo Mercuriali

Conducted by Lovro von Matacic
Orchestra e Coro del Teatro alla Scala Milano
Chorus Master: Norberto Mola

The Performers

∞

FRANCO CORELLI (Turiddu in *Cavalleria Rusticana*/Canio (Pagliaccio) in *I Pagliacci)* was the most charismatic Italian tenor of his generation—tall and handsome, possessed with a powerful and incandescent voice, a performer who delivered onstage and in the recording studio with an almost ferocious intensity. Born in 1921 in Ancona, Italy, Corelli trained as a naval architect before entering the Pesaro Conservatory to study voice in 1947. He soon quit the conservatory, losing patience with the nature of academic training, and taught himself operatic roles by listening to recordings of great singers. For whatever hurdles it may have created for him as a working musician, this unorthodox development resulted in an extraordinary singing style that was evident in his professional debut at the Spoleto Festival in 1952, as Don José in *Carmen.* The basic sound of Corelli's voice was immediately arresting in its propulsive brilliance and its expressive commitment. He sang with a beautiful sense of line, often creating a beautiful, even poetic impression. But it was intensity that defined his style, and his passion as a performer seemed, to some observers, to verge on hysteria. His high notes, over which he fretted and worried for his whole career, were miraculous both in their vibrant, full-bodied power and in his ability to control them. Corelli made his debut at La Scala, Milan, in 1954, after a brief stint with provincial Italian companies, and became a star there, as well as at the Maggio Musicale Fiorentino (Florence May Festival) and in the outdoor performances at the Arena di Verona. Highlights of Corelli's repertoire included, in addition to Don José, Canio in *I Pagliacci,* Turridu in *Cavalleria Rusticana,* Radames in *Aida,* Don Alvaro in *La Forza del Destino,* Manrico in *Il Trovatore,* Pollione in *Norma,* Cavaradossi in *Tosca,* Roméo in Gounod's *Roméo et Juliette,* and Calaf in *Turandot,* as well as the title roles in *Andrea Chénier, Ernani,* and *Werther.* International debuts throughout the 1950s—at the Vienna Staatsoper, the Paris Opéra, Covent Garden in London and, in the U.S., in San Francisco and Chicago—established him as the most exciting tenor in a generation that also included Mario del Monaco, Richard Tucker, and Giuseppe di Stefano. Corelli's Metropolitan Opera debut in *Il Trovatore* came the same legendary night as Leontyne Price's. Though some critics derided Corelli for the unabashed intensity of his performances, he was a brilliant exponent of a dramatic Italian vocal style that very nearly disappeared after his retirement in the early 1970s. He never masked how difficult, psychologically and emotionally, he found the process of performing, which may be the reason he retired from singing while his voice was still in excellent condition. Despite the vogue for more lyrical tenor singing that came with the popularity of Luciano Pavarotti and Plácido Domingo, Corelli has re-emerged through recordings and recently rediscovered videos as one of the most admired tenors of the century.

VICTORIA DE LOS ANGELES (Santuzza in *Cavalleria Rusticana*) is one of the most beloved singers of the second half of the 20th century. The Spanish soprano made her debut in 1944 in her native Barcelona and continued to win a unique acclaim in opera, concert and song for the next 50 years. Throughout the 1950s, she made a series of important operatic debuts in Paris, London, New York, Vienna and other international capitals that highlighted her unique charm in age that also featured such strikingly gifted sopranos as Maria Callas, Renata Tebaldi, Elisabeth Schwarzkopf and Lisa Della Casa. "For sheer quality of sound, Victoria's [voice] affects me more than any other," the legendary accompanist Gerald Moore once wrote. De Los Angeles possessed one of the most instantly affecting voices of her time, with a sound that seemed to combine angelic purity and sensuous allure. She enjoyed a career of remarkable breadth and depth. Her prime years in opera came in the 1950s and early 1960s, in such demanding roles as the title characters in Massenet's *Manon* and Puccini's *Madama Butterfly,* and as Elisabeth in Wagner's Tannhäuser, as well as the great heroines of the Italian, French and Spanish repertoire. De Los Angeles also enjoyed a prolific international recording career which preserved her unforgettable portrayals of Mélisande in Debussy's *Pélleas et Mélisande,* Mimì in *La Bohème,* Marguerite in *Faust* and—though she rarely sang it onstage—her uniquely elegant interpretation of *Carmen.* After retiring from the stage in 1969, she continued to be greatly admired as a recitalist. She has done more than any artist to bring into the mainstream the richly varied song literature of her native Spain, from ancient Sephardic songs to the work of 20th-century composers.

JON VICKERS IN REHEARSAL AT COVENT GARDEN AS CANIO IN I PAGLIACCI, 1959.

De Los Angeles was also acclaimed her many recitals and recordings of German lieder and French *melodie.*

MARIO SERENI (Alfio in *Cavalleria Rusticana*) enjoyed great popularity in the 1950s and 1960s in the important baritone roles of the Italian repertoire, both in major international houses and on recordings. Born in Perugia, Italy, in 1928, Sereni attended Rome's Accademia de Santa Cecilia and the Accademia Chigiana in Siena, where he was the student of Mario Basiola. His professional career began in 1953 on an unusually high level — at the Maggio Musicale Fiorentino (Florence May Festival) — and within four years, he had made his Metropolitan Opera debut (as Gérard in *Andrea Chénier*) and had also sung at Buenos Aires' Teatro Colón. Sereni enjoyed a long and steady career at the Met, London's Covent Garden, Milan's La Scala, the Vienna Staatsoper and other companies around the world. Despite his success, Sereni remained in the shadow of more charismatic baritones of his time — principally Leonard Warren Tito Gobbi, Robert Merrill, Ettore Bastianini, Piero Cappuccilli and Rolando Panerai — and critics of the time were frequently dismissive of his singing. Yet his many recordings (he can be heard on the legendary "Lisbon *Traviata*" recording of 1958 with Maria Callas and Alfredo Kraus) reveal a singer and musician of considerable distinction, with a handsome voice, a durable technique and a fine sense of style.

LUCINE AMARA (Nedda in *Pagliacci*) spent much of her career as one of the Metropolitan Opera's most reliable and admired sopranos, beginning with her debut in 1950 as the Celestial Voice in the production of *Don Carlo* that inaugurated Rudolf Bing's tenure as the company's general manager. Born Lucine

Armaganian in Hartford, Connecticut, in 1927, she began her vocal studies in San Francisco, after her family moved to the West Coast. She made her professional debuts there, first as a member of the San Francisco Opera Chorus, and in 1947 failed to impress the management of the Metropolitan Opera when she auditioned. Amara continued to study at University of Southern California and made her debut with the San Francisco Symphony Orchestra under Pierre Monteux. She also appeared in a movie during this time, opposite Mario Lanza in *The Great Caruso.* Her Met debut led to a series of small roles until the 1952-53 season, when she created a sensation in the role of Nedda. Thereafter, she became a mainstay of the Met roster until the late 1970s. Amara also sang with the Glyndebourne Festival (the title role in *Ariadne auf Naxos* in 1957) and the Vienna State Opera (as Nedda and in the title role of *Aida*). Among her recordings is the classic Beecham/Bjoerling/de Los Angeles *La Bohème,* on which she sings the role of Musetta. Her Met career included hundreds of performances in the great soprano roles of the Italian, French and Russian repertoire, though it ended with controversy, when she sued the company for age discrimination.

TITO GOBBI (Tonio in *Pagliacci*) won acclaim around the world as perhaps the finest singing actor of his day. The Italian baritone, born near Venice in 1913, has been immortalized through his mesmerizing portrayal of the villainous Baron Scarpia in two recordings and video excerpts from *Tosca* with soprano Maria Callas. Though his powerful and arresting voice lacked perhaps the supple richness of his contemporaries Gino Bechi, Robert Merrill and Leonard Warren, his interpretive skills were without equal. The result was a gallery of great performances in the title roles of *Don Giovanni, Rigoletto* and *Falstaff,* as Figaro in *The Barber of Seville,* Renato in *Un ballo in maschera,* Germont in *La*

TITO GOBBI AS BARON
SCARPIA IN PUCCINI'S
TOSCA

Traviata and other key roles in the Italian repertoire such as Tonio. Gobbi made his professional debut in 1935 in Gubbio as Rodolfo in *La Sonnambula,* and appeared at La Scala in a bit part in the premiere of Pizzetti's *Oreseolo* during the 1935-36 season. His first significant performances in leading roles came in Rome in the late 1930s, and his career continued to grow as he sang throughout Italy and on Italian radio during World War II. Gobbi sang his first Scarpia in 1940 and made a formal debut at La Scala in 1942 as Belcore in *L'elisir d'amore.* Following the war, his international career quickly began to unfold with debuts in Stockholm, San Francisco, London and Chicago. His Metropolitan Opera debut, in 1956, was as Scarpia, a role he recorded so memorably with Maria Callas as Tosca in 1953. They actually did not perform Puccini's opera together until Callas' final round of stage appearances in the mid-1960s, portions of which were captured on film. The footage reveals Gobbi to be the consummate master of operatic performance. Though he retired from the stage in 1979, he remained active as a stage director until his death in 1984. Gobbi was the brother-in-law of the celebrated bass Boris Christoff, with whom he frequently performed.

GABRIELE SANTINI provided a fascinating link in the performance of Italian opera, having been born in 1886 and beginning his career in the shadow of such key figures as Puccini, Mascagni and Toscanini. A native of Perugia, Santini studied there and in Bologna before beginning his career as conductor in locales as far-flung as Rio de Janeiro, Buenos Aires, Chicago and New York. From 1925 until 1929, he served as Toscanini's assistant at La Scala in Milan, and later served as a conductor and eventually artistic director of the Rome Opera. Santini made a number of recordings of complete operas. He died in Rome in 1964.

LOVRO VON MATACIC enjoyed a long association with EMI, for which he conducted a number of opera and operetta recordings. The Yugoslavian native was born in 1899 and studied at the Vienna Conservatory. He made his professional debut in 1919 in Cologne before returning to his homeland for a series of positions in Ljubljana, Belgrade and Zagreb. Von Matacic served as principal conductor of the Belgrade Opera (1938-42), followed by a stint at the Vienna Volksoper (1942-45). After World War II, he conducted throughout Europe, holding a succession of jobs as music director or principal conductor of the Dresden State Opera, Frankfurt Opera, Zagreb Philharmonic and Monte Carlo Opera. Von Matacic also guest-conducted throughout Europe, South America and the U.S. He died in 1985 in Zagreb.

FILM DIRECTOR FRANCO ZEFFIRELLI WORKS WITH PLACIDO DOMINGO AND ELENA OBRASTSOVA AT LA SCALA, MILAN. (CAVALLERIA RUSTICANA)

The Libretto

Cavalleria Rusticana

Act One

PRELUDE

disc no. 1
tracks 1-3
O Lola ch'hai di latti la cammisa (Turiddu's Serenade) The orchestra describes the fragrant calm of an Easter Sunday morning in rural Sicily. But the passion that swiftly emerges, followed by a sudden crescendo, suggests that anguish lurks within the sunny stillness. A plaintive melody **(01:14)** is heard, the melody with which Santuzza later will insist to the indifferent Turiddu that she loves him. It gathers in intensity, only to be shocked into silence by the distant sound of a harp and the voice of Turiddu **(Track 2)** in a brief, passionate serenade to Lola. The orchestra returns **(Track 3)**, virtually where it left off, as if to mourn for the forgotten Santuzza. An angry outburst is followed by a sorrowful statement of music that will reappear in her confrontation with Turiddu. It swells passionately **(02:02)**, then fades into quiet grief and resignation.

A public square in a village in Sicily. In the rear, to the right a church, to the left a tavern and the house of Mamma Lucia. It is Easter morning. The curtain is lowered.

TURIDDU

Lola ch'hai di latti la cammisa
Sì bianca e russa comu la cirasa,
Quannu t'affacci fai la vucca a risa,
Biatu cui ti dà lu primmu vasu! Ntra la
puorta tua lu suangu è sparsu, Ma nun me
mpuorta si ce muoru accisu...
E se iddu muoru e vaju'n paradisu Si nun
ce truovo a ttia, mancu ce trasu.

TURIDDU

Oh, Lola of the milk-white blouse,
of the fair skin and cherry lips,
when you come laughing to the window,
happy is he who first can kiss you.
Blood has been shed across your door:
but I shall not care if I am slain there...
And if I should die and go to Paradise,
and not find you there, I would not stay.

Prelude (conclusion)

(The curtain rises. The stage is empty.)

CORO DI DONNE *(di dentro)*

Gli aranci olezzano
Sui verdi margini,
Cantan le allodole
Tra i mirti in fior;
Tempo è si mormori
Da ognuno il tenero
Canto che i palpiti
Raddoppia al cor.

CHORUS OF WOMEN *(within)*

The green meadows,
are fragrant with orange,
the larks sing
in the flowering myrtle;
now is the time for all
to sing the tender strain
that quickens the beat
of hearts in Spring.

CORO DI UOMINI *(di dentro)*

In mezzo al campo tra le spiche d'oro
Giunge il rumore delle vostre spole,
Noi stanchi riposando dal lavoro
A voi pensiamo, o belle occhi-di-sole.
O belle occhi-di-sole, a voi corriamo,
Come vola l'augello al suo richiamo.

CHORUS OF MEN *(within)*

The hum of your shuttles reaches us
in the fields amid the golden corn,
and we think of you, eyes bright as sun,
as weary we rest from our labours.
Oh eyes bright as sun, we fly to you,
as the bird flies, answering its call.

(The members of the chorus enter, a few at a time.)

CORO DI DONNE
Cessin le rustiche
Opre; la Vergine
Serena allietasi Del Salvator;
Tempo è si mormori
Da ognuno il tenero
Canto che i palpiti
Raddoppia al cor.

CHORUS OF WOMEN
Now in the fields
let labour cease; serenely,
the Virgin rejoices in the Saviour;
now is the time for all
to sing the tender strain
that quickens the beat
of hearts in Spring.

CORO DI UOMINI
In mezzo al campo, ecc.

CHORUS OF MEN
The hum of your shuttles, etc.

(The chorus crosses the stage and leaves. Mamma Lucia comes out of her house; Santuzza enters from the right.)

SANTUZZA
Dite, Mamma Lucia...

SANTUZZA
Tell me, Mamma Lucia...

MAMMA LUCIA *(sorpresa)*
Sei tu? Che vuoi?

MAMMA LUCIA *(surprised)*
It's you? What do you want?

SANTUZZA
Turiddu ov'è?

SANTUZZA
Where is Turiddu?

MAMMA LUCIA
Fin qui vieni a cercare
Il figlio mio?

MAMMA LUCIA
So you come even here
looking for my son?

SANTUZZA
Voglio saper soltanto,
Perdonatemi voi, dove trovarlo.

SANTUZZA
Forgive me, I only want to know
where I can find him.

MAMMA LUCIA
Non lo so, non lo so, non voglio brighe.

SANTUZZA
Mamma Lucia, vi supplico piangendo,
Fate come il Signore a Maddalena,
Ditemi per pietà, dov'è Turiddu.

MAMMA LUCIA
È andato per il vino a Francofonte.

SANTUZZA
No! l'han visto in paese ad alta notte.

MAMMA LUCIA
Che dici? Se non è tornato a casa!

(going towards her doorway)

Entra.

SANTUZZA *(disperata)*
Non posso entrare in casa vostra...
Sono scomunicata!

MAMMA LUCIA
E che ne sai del mio figliuolo?

SANTUZZA
Quale spina ho in core!

MAMMA LUCIA
I'm sure I don't know. I don't want trouble.

SANTUZZA
Mamma Lucia, I beg you with my tears.
Do as our Lord did with the Magdalen,
have pity and tell me, where is Turiddu?

MAMMA LUCIA
He's gone to Francofonte to get wine.

SANTUZZA
No! They saw him here in the village late
last night.

MAMMA LUCIA
What's that? But he did not come home!

Come in.

SANTUZZA *(desperately)*
I cannot enter your house...
I have been excommunicated!

MAMMA LUCIA
And what do you know about my son?

SANTUZZA
What a sharp pain I have about my heart!

(Alfio enters, followed by the chorus.)

Il cavallo scalpita The arrival in the square of the teamster Alfio (actually signaled at **4:08** in **Track 5**) is heralded by the crack of his whip and the jangle of bridle bells, over a brusque figure in the orchestra. With a swaggering self-confidence reflected in a blunt, striding melody, Alfio sings of the exuberance of his work **(00:02)**, and the crowd in the square agrees **(00:31)**. Then the music slows suggestively **(00:58)** when he begins to sing of his faithful wife Lola waiting for him, only to quicken again **(01:26)** when he returns to the subject of his work, which the crowd cheers.

ALFIO
Il cavallo scalpita,
I sonagli squillano,
Schiocchi la frusta. Ehi là!
Soffi il vento gelido,
Cada l'acqua e nevichi,
A me che cosa fa?

CORO
O che bel mestiere
Fare il carrettiere,
Andar di qua e di là!

ALFIO
M'aspetta a casa Lola
Che m'ama e mi consola,
Ch'è tutta fedeltà.
Il cavallo scalpiti,
I sonagli squillino,
È Pasqua, ed io son qua!

CORO
O che bel mestiere.
Fare il carrettiere,
Andar di qua e di là!

ALFIO
The horse stamps,
the bridle-bells jingle,
the whip cracks. Ho-la!
Let freezing winds blow,
let it rain, let it snow,
what should I care?

CHORUS
Oh what a fine trade
that of a carter,
travelling here and there!

ALFIO
At home Lola awaits me,
my love and my comfort
who is all faithfulness.
So let the horse stamp
and the bridle-bells jingle.
It's Easter, and I am here.

CHORUS
Oh what a fine trade
that of a carter,
travelling here and there!

RENATA TEBALDI, ONE OF
THE MOST IMPORTANT
SINGERS TO SING SANTUZZA
IN CAVALLERIA RUSTICANA.

MAMMA LUCIA
Beato voi, compar Alfio, che siete
Sempre allegro così!

ALFIO
Mamma Lucia,
N'avete ancora di quel vecchio vino?

MAMMA LUCIA
Non so; Turiddu è andato a
provvederne.

ALFIO
Se è sempre qui!
L'ho visto stamattina vicino a casa mia.

MAMMA LUCIA *(sorpresa)*
Come?

SANTUZZA *(rapidamente)*
Tacete.

(The Hallelujah is heard from the church.)

ALFIO
Io me ne vado; ite voi altre in chiesa.

(Alfio leaves.)

MAMMA LUCIA
How lucky you are, good Alfio,
to be always so merry!

ALFIO
Mamma Lucia,
do you have any more of that old wine?

MAMMA LUCIA
I don't know. Turiddu has gone to get
some.

ALFIO
But he is still here!
I saw him this morning near my house.

MAMMA LUCIA *(surprised)*
What?

SANTUZZA *(quickly)*
Be quiet.

ALFIO
I'm going along. You others go to church.

**disc no. 1
tracks 8&9**

Regina Coeli...Ineggiamo, Il Signore non è morto From within
the church, the choir is heard singing a gentle setting of the Regina Coeli. In the
square, Easter worshippers sing in hushed response **(00:47)**. At the sound of
the organ within the church **(01:49)**, Santuzza is deeply moved. She begins to
sing a passionate hymn **(Track 9)**, which the worshippers take up, and it grows
in fervor. When they finish, the choir in the church can be heard **(02:14)**.
Santuzza all but weeps as she and the crowd offer a final prayer to God.
The crowd enters the church, but Santuzza cannot; as the organ plays again

(03:19), she is left alone in the square as Mamma Lucia enters to ask her why she is trying to keep information from Alfio.

CORO *(dalla chiesa)*
Regina Coeli, laetare; Alleluja!
Quia, quem meruisti portare; Alleluja!
Resurrexit sicut dixit; Alleluja!

CORO *(in piazza)*
Inneggiamo, il Signor non è morto,
Ei fulgente ha dischiuso l'avel,
Inneggiamo, al Signore risorto,
Oggi asceso alla gloria del Ciel!

SANTUZZA E CORO
Inneggiamo, il Signor non è morto,
Inneggiamo, al Signore risorto,
Oggi asceso alla gloria del Ciel,
Ei fulgente ha dischiuso l'avel!

CHORUS *(from within the church)*
Regina Coeli, laetare; Alleluia!
Quia, quem meruisti portare; Alleluia!
Resurrexit sicut dixit; Alleluia!

CHORUS *(in the square)*
Let us sing His praise, the Lord is not dead,
resplendent, He has spread His wings,
let us sing His praise, the Lord has risen
and today ascended to the glory of Heaven!

SANTUZZA AND CHORUS
Let us sing His praise, the Lord is not dead,
let us sing His praise, the Lord has risen
and today ascended to the glory of Heaven!
Resplendent, He has spread His wings.

(The chorus leaves slowly. Santuzza and Mamma Lucia remain alone.)

MAMMA LUCIA
Perché m'hai fatto segno di tacere?

MAMMA LUCIA
Why did you motion me to be quiet?

disc no. 1/track 10 *Voi lo sapete, o mamma* The desolate orchestral introduction says it all: Santuzza has a pitiful story to tell Mamma Lucia. The aria is unfolds freely, rising intensity on a repeated cry from Santuzza on the word "l'amai" (I loved him) **(01:27)**, followed by restatement of the aria's introduction. Instead of repeating anything, a bitter urgency is heard in a new melodic strain **(01:56)** as Santuzza describes Lola. But Santuzza's repeated cry that Lola took Turiddu from her **(02:28)** leads her back into her own self-pity. Mamma Lucia is aghast **(03:21)**, and Santuzza answers, with a cry, that her own plight has left her a damned woman **(03:31)**. But a gentle turn in the music leads to Santuzza's suggestion that Mamma Lucia pray for her **(03:54)**, in the hope that she can convince Turiddu to take her back. Mamma Lucia immediately turns toward the church, muttering a prayer **(04:38)** as Santuzza is, once again, left alone.

SANTUZZA

Voi lo sapete, o mamma, prima d'andar soldato Turiddu aveva a Lola eterna fè giurato.
Tornò, la seppe sposa, e con un nuovo amoreVolle spegner la fiamma che gli bruciava il core.
M'amò,
l'amai. Quell'invida d'ogni delizia mia, Del suo sposo dimentica, arse di gelosia Me l'ha rapito. Priva dell'onor mio rimango;
Lola e Turiddu s'amano, io piango, io piango!

MAMMA LUCIA

Miseri noi, che cosa vieni a dirmi
In questo santo giorno?

SANTUZZA

Io son dannata...
Andate, o mamma, ad implorare Iddio,
E pregate per me...Verrà Turiddu,
Vo' supplicarlo un'altra volta ancora!

MAMMA LUCIA (avviandosi alla chiesa)
Aiutatela voi, Santa Maria!

SANTUZZA

You know well, Mamma, that before he left as a soldier Turiddu pledged eternal faith to Lola.
He returned and found her married, and with a new love he sought to quench the fire of his ancient passion.
He loved me:
I loved him. And she, who burned with jealousy, envying my slightest joy, forgetting her husband, she snatched him from me. And so I am dishonoured and bereft. They love each other! And I weep alone!

MAMMA LUCIA

Merciful Heaven! What horrors do you come to tell me on this holy day?

SANTUZZA

I am damned...
Oh mamma, go and pray to God, entreat him for me...Turiddu will be coming and once again I want to plead with him!

MAMMA LUCIA (going towards the church)
Help her, Holy Mary!

(Mamma Lucia goes out, Turiddu enters.)

TURIDDU
Tu qui, Santuzza?

SANTUZZA
Qui t'aspettavo.

TURIDDU
È Pasqua, in chiesa non vai?

SANTUZZA
Non vò. Debbo parlarti...

TURIDDU
Mamma cercavo.

SANTUZZA
Debbo parlarti...

TURIDDU
Qui no! Qui no!

SANTUZZA
Dove sei stato?

TURIDDU
Che vuoi tu dire?
A Francofonte!

SANTUZZA
No, non è ver!

TURIDDU
Santuzza, credimi...

TURIDDU
You here, Santuzza?

SANTUZZA
I was waiting for you.

TURIDDU
You're not going to church on Easter?

SANTUZZA
No, I must talk to you...

TURIDDU
I was looking for mamma...

SANTUZZA
I must talk to you...

TURIDDU
Not here! Not here!

SANTUZZA
Where have you been?

TURIDDU
What do you mean?
In Francofonte!

SANTUZZA
No, that's not true!

TURIDDU
Believe me, Santuzza...

SANTUZZA
No, non mentire;
Ti vidi volger giù dal sentier.
E stamattina, all'alba, t'hanno scorto
Presso l'uscio di Lola.

TURIDDU
Ah! Mi hai spiato!

SANTUZZA
No, te lo giuro. A noi l'ha raccontato
Compar Alfio, il marito, poco fa.

TURIDDU
Così ricambi l'amor che ti porto?
Vuoi che m'uccida?

SANTUZZA
Oh! Questo non lo dire!

TURIDDU
Lasciami dunque, lasciami,
invan tenti sopire Il giusto sdegno colla tua
pietà.

SANTUZZA
Tu l'ami, dunque?

TURIDDU
No...

SANTUZZA
Assai più bella è Lola.

TURIDDU
Taci, non l'amo.

SANTUZZA
No, don't lie;
I saw you turn down from the path.
And this morning, at dawn,
they saw you near Lola's door.

TURIDDU
So! You've been spying on me!

SANTUZZA
No, I swear! It was her husband Alfio
who told us that just now.

TURIDDU
And this is how you repay my love?
Do you want him to kill me?

SANTUZZA
Oh, no! Don't say that!

TURIDDU
Let me be, then! Leave me! It's futile your
trying to use your wretchedness to appease
my anger!

SANTUZZA
You love her, then?

TURIDDU
No...

SANTUZZA
Lola is much more beautiful.

TURIDDU
Be quiet, I don't love her.

PLACIDO DOMINGO

SANTUZZA
L'ami...Oh, maledetta!

TURIDDU
Santuzza!

SANTUZZA
Quella cattiva femmina ti tolse a me!

TURIDDU
Bada, Santuzza, schiavo non sono
Di questa vana tua gelosia!

SANTUZZA
Battimi, insultami, t'amo e perdono,
Ma è troppo forte l'angoscia mia...

LOLA (*fuori scena*)
Fior di giaggiolo,
Gli angioli belli stanno a mille in cielo,
Ma bello come lui ce n'è uno solo.

(*Lola enters.*)

Oh! Turiddu, è passato Alfio?

TURIDDU (*impacciato*)
Sono giunto ora in piazza. Non so.

LOLA (*ironica*)
Forse è rimasto dal maniscalco,
ma non può tardare.
E voi sentite le funzioni in piazza?

SANTUZZA
You love her...Oh, damned woman!

TURIDDU
Santuzza!

SANTUZZA
That wicked woman took you from me!

TURIDDU
Take care, Santuzza, I'm not the slave
of this vain jealousy of yours.

SANTUZZA
Beat me, insult me, I love you and forgive you...
But anguish overwhelms me...

LOLA (*from without*)
O blossoming iris!
Thousands of beautiful angels there are in Heaven, but there is only one as beautiful as he.

Oh! Turiddu, has Alfio been by?

TURIDDU (*embarrassed*)
I came here just now. I don't know.

LOLA (*ironically*)
Perhaps he's stayed at the blacksmith's,
but he can't be long.
And so you are hearing Mass in the square?

TURIDDU
Santuzza mi narrava...

SANTUZZA *(tetra)*
Gli dicevo che oggi è Pasqua
E il Signor vede ogni cosa!

LOLA *(ironica)*
Non venite alla messa?

SANTUZZA *(tetra)*
Io no, ci deve andar chi sa di
non aver peccato...

LOLA
Io ringrazio il Signore e bacio in terra!

SANTUZZA *(con amarezza)*
Oh! Fate bene, Lola!

TURIDDU
Andiamo! Andiamo!
Qui non abbiam che fare.

LOLA *(ironica)*
Oh, rimanete!

SANTUZZA *(a Turiddu)*
Sì, resta, resta, ho da parlarti ancora!

LOLA
E v'assista il Signore, io me ne vado.

(Lola goes into the church.)

TURIDDU
Santuzza was telling me...

SANTUZZA *(darkly)*
I was telling him that today is Easter
and that the Lord sees all things!

LOLA *(ironically)*
Aren't you coming to Mass?

SANTUZZA *(darkly)*
Not I. Only those may go who know
they have not sinned.

LOLA
I give thanks to the Lord and kiss the earth!

SANTUZZA *(bitterly)*
Oh! You do well, Lola!

TURIDDU
Come on! Let's go!
We have nothing to do here.

LOLA *(ironically)*
Oh, do stay!

SANTUZZA *(to Turiddu)*
Yes, stay, stay, for I have more to say to
you.

LOLA
And the Lord help you...I am going.

TURIDDU *(irato)*
Ah! Lo vedi, che hai tu detto?...

SANTUZZA
L'hai voluto, e ben ti sta.

TURIDDU *(le s'avventa)*
Ah! Per Dio!

SANTUZZA
Squarciami il petto!...

TURIDDU *(avviandosi)*
No!

SANTUZZA *(trattenendolo)*
Turiddu, ascolta!

TURIDDU
Va!

TURIDDU *(furious)*
Ah! You see? What have you said?

SANTUZZA
You wanted it, and it serves you right.

TURIDDU *(rushing towards her)*
Ah! By God!

SANTUZZA
Tear my heart out!...

TURIDDU *(turning to go)*
No!

SANTUZZA *(detaining him)*
Turiddu, listen!

TURIDDU
Go!

disc no. 1/track 14 *No, no, Turiddu* Santuzza's confrontation with Turiddu is going nowhere, so she begins to plead with him, through the anguished melodies heard in the opera's prelude. He could not be less interested, his disgust as intense as her passion. Their confrontation almost erupts when Santuzza breaks off **(02:28)** and literally begs him on her knees. But their feelings are too fierce **(03:25)**, and they are once again berating each other when Turiddu physically shoves her to the ground **(03:41)**. A vicious exchange between them results in Santuzza's enraged curse **(03:52)**, which she shrieks at him as walks away, leaving her shattered and weeping.

SANTUZZA
Turiddu, ascolta!
No, no, Turiddu, rimani, rimani ancora,
Abbandonarmi dunque tu vuoi?

SANTUZZA
Turiddu, listen!
No, no, Turiddu, stay with me, stay,
would you abandon me so?

TURIDDU
Perché seguirmi, perché spiarmi
Sul limitare fin della chiesa?

SANTUZZA
La tua Santuzza piange e t'implora;
Come cacciarla così tu puoi?

TURIDDU
Va, ti ripeto, va, non tediarmi;
Pentirsi è vano...dopo l'offesa.

SANTUZZA (*minacciosa*)
Bada!

TURIDDU
Dell'ira tua non mi curo!

(He throws her to the ground and runs into the church.)

SANTUZZA (*nel colmo dell'ira*)
A te la mala Pasqua, spergiuro!

(Alfio enters.)

SANTUZZA
Oh! Il Signore vi manda,
compar Alfio!

ALFIO
A che punto è la messa?

SANTUZZA
È tardi ormai ma per voi,
Lola è andata con Turiddu!

TURIDDU
Why do you pursue me, why spy on me
even on the threshold of the church?

SANTUZZA
Your Santuzza implores you with her tears:
how can you drive her away like this?

TURIDDU
Go, I tell you, go, and don't pester me;
it is useless to repent...after the offence.

SANTUZZA (*threatening*)
Take care!

TURIDDU
I can't be bothered with your raging!

SANTUZZA (*in the height of fury*)
An evil Easter to you, betrayer!

SANTUZZA
Oh! The Lord sends you this way, neighbour Alfio!

ALFIO
Where are they in the Mass?

SANTUZZA
Almost over...but there is this for you:
Lola went off with Turiddu!

ALFIO
Che avete detto?

SANTUZZA
Che mentre correte all'acqua e al vento
A guadagnarvi il pane,
Lola v'adorna il tetto in malo modo!

ALFIO
Ah! Nel nome di Dio, Santa,
che dite?

SANTUZZA
Il ver. Turiddu mi tolse l'onore,
E vostra moglie lui rapiva a me!

ALFIO
Se voi mentite, vo' schiantarvi il core!

SANTUZZA
Uso a mentire il labbro mio non è!
Per la vergogna mia, pel mio dolore,
La triste verità vi dissi, ahimè!

ALFIO
Comare Santa, allor grato vi sono.

SANTUZZA
Infame io son che vi parlai così!

ALFIO
Infami loro, ad essi non perdono,
Vendetta avrò pria che tramonti il dì!
Io sangue voglio, all'ira m'abbandono,
In odio tutto l'amor mio finì!

ALFIO
What did you say?

SANTUZZA
I said that while you toil in rain
and wind, to earn your bread,
Lola betrays you with another man!

ALFIO
Ah! In God's name, Santa, what are you
saying!

SANTUZZA
The simple truth. Turiddu dishonoured
me, and your wife stole him from me.

ALFIO
If you are lying, I'll tear out your heart!

SANTUZZA
My lips are not used to lying.
To my shame and to my sorrow,
it is the awful truth I've told you!

ALFIO
Then neighbour Santa, I am grateful to
you.

SANTUZZA
Oh, how base I am to have told you this!

ALFIO
How base are they!...And them I'll not forgive! I will have vengeance before this day
is over. I want their blood, I revel in wrath.
All my love has ended now in hatred!

(Santuzza and Alfio go out.)

disc no. 1/track 16 *Intermezzo* The most famous passage in the score, the orchestral Intermezzo brings some relief from the tension of the story. The strings tenderly repeat the Regina Coeli melody heard earlier from the church choir. A boldly passionate, grieving melody sings out **(01:28)**, supported by the organ and harp, and breaking into sobs **(02:20)** before fading away.

(The Mass is over, all emerge from the church. Mamma Lucia crosses the square and goes into her house. Lola, Turiddu and the chorus remain on stage.)

CORO DI UOMINI
A casa, a casa, amici, ove ci aspettano
Le nostre donne, andiam,
Or che letizia rasserena gli animi
Senza indugio corriam.

CORO DI DONNE
A casa, a casa, amiche, ove ci aspettano
I nostri sposi, andiam,
Or che letizia rasserena gli animi
Senza indugio corriam.

TURIDDU *(a Lola, che s'avvia)*
Comare Lola, ve ne andate via
Senza nemmeno salutare?

LOLA
Vado a casa; non ho visto compar Alfio.

TURIDDU
Non ci pensate, verrà in piazza.

(to the chorus)

CHORUS OF MEN
Let's go home, friends, let's hurry home,
where our wives await us,
now that gladness fills our hearts,
come, let's not tarry.

CHORUS OF WOMEN
Let's go home, friends, let's hurry home,
where our husbands await us,
now that gladness fills our hearts,
come, let's not tarry.

TURIDDU *(to Lola, who is about to leave)*
Neighbour Lola, are you leaving
without even saying good-bye?

LOLA
I'm going home. I have not seen Alfio.

TURIDDU
Don't worry about that, he'll be along.

Intanto amici, qua, beviamone un bicchiere.

And meanwhile, friends, let's drink a glass together!

(All gather around the table at the tavern to take glasses.)

disc no. 1/track 20 *Viva il vino spumeggiante* Unaware that he is a marked man, Turiddu sings this vibrant little drinking song to his friends, with interjections **(01:08)** from the guests and, particularly, Lola. The crowd takes up the melody of Turiddu's song **(01:38)**, followed by a festive coda **(02:13)**.

Viva il vino spumeggiante
Nel bicchiere scintillante
Come il riso dell'amante
Mite infonde il giubilo!
Viva il vino ch'è sincero,
Che ci allieta ogni pensiero,
E che affoga l'umor nero
Nell'ebbrezza tenera.

Here's to sparkling wine
in glittering glasses,
wine that awakens joy
like a lover's laughter.
Here's to the wine that is pure,
that awakens the heart to rapture,
and in gay abandon
drowns each sombre thought.

CORO
Viva!

CHORUS
Cheers!

TURIDDU *(a Lola)*
Ai vostri amori!

TURIDDU *(to Lola)*
To your loves!

LOLA *(a Turiddu)*
Alla fortuna vostra!

LOLA *(to Turiddu)*
To your good fortune!

TURIDDU
Beviam!
CORO
Beviam! Rinnovisi la giostra!
Viva il vino spumeggiante, ecc.

TURIDDU
Let's drink!

CHORUS
Let's drink! Let's fill again!
Here's to sparkling wine, etc.

(Alfio enters.)

ALFIO
A voi tutti, salute!

CORO
Compar Alfio, salute!

TURIDDU
Benvenuto! Con noi dovete bere.

(He hands him a glass.)

Ecco, pieno è il bicchiere.

ALFIO *(respingendolo)*
Grazie, ma il vostro vino io non l'accetto,
Diverrebbe veleno entro il mio petto!

TURIDDU *(gettando via il vino)*
A piacer vostro!

LOLA
Ahimè! Che mai sarà?

ALCUNE DONNE *(a Lola)*
Comare Lola, andiamo via di quà

. *(The entire chorus leave, escorting Lola.)*

TURIDDU
Avete altro da dirmi?

ALFIO
Io? Nulla!

TURIDDU
Allora sono agli ordini vostri.

ALFIO
Good health to you all!

CHORUS
And to you, neighbour Alfio!

TURIDDU
Welcome! You must drink a toast with us!

Here, your glass is full.

ALFIO *(rejecting it)*
Thanks, but I do not accept your wine:
it would turn to poison in my breast!

TURIDDU *(throwing the wine away)*
Just as you wish!

LOLA
Alas! What can this mean?

SOME WOMEN *(to Lola)*
Neighbour Lola, let's go away from here.

TURIDDU
Do you have anything else to say to me?

ALFIO
I? nothing?

TURIDDU
Then I am at your service.

ALFIO
Or ora!

ALFIO
At once, then!

TURIDDU
Or ora!

TURIDDU
At once!

(The two men embrace, in the manner prescribed by ritual, and Turiddu bites Alfio's right ear.)

ALFIO
Compar Turiddu, avete morso a buono!
C'intenderemo bene, a quel che pare!

ALFIO
Neighbour Turiddu, you have bitten hard and well:and as I see, we'll understand each other perfectly!

TURIDDU
Compar Alfio...
Lo so che il torto è mio,
E ve lo giuro nel nome di Dio
Che al par d'un cane mi farei sgozzar;
Ma, s'io non vivo, resta abbandonata
Povera Santa, lei che mi s'è data!
Vi saprò in core il ferro mio piantar!

TURIDDU
Neighbour Alfio...
I know that I am in the wrong,
and in God's name I swear to you
that I'd let you kill me like a dog...
Except that, if I die, Santa is left alone,
Santa is abandoned, who gave herself to me! So I'll know how to plant my knife within your heart!

ALFIO *(freddamente)*
Compare, fate come più vi piace;
Io v'aspetto qui fuori, dietro l'orto.

ALFIO *(icily)*
Neighbour, do as you see fit:
I'll wait for you down there, beyond the garden.

(Alfio goes out. Mamma Lucia enters.)

disc no. 1/track 20 *Mamma, quel vino è generoso* Against an urgent tremolo in the violins, Turiddu—well aware of what he faces—sings to Mamma Lucia of his regret at drinking too much heady wine. He will go for fresh air, he tells her, but first **(00:51)** he asks her to bless him as she did when he went to the army. His sense of foreboding is reflected in the gravity of the music as he begs her to be a mother to Santuzza **(01:47)** if he does not return. Mamma Lucia does not understand, and Turiddu presses her to pray for him **(02:43)** before they embrace for the last time. As he leaves, Mamma Lucia tries to follow when Santuzza re- enters. But the happy reunion of the two women is shortlived: from the distance, one of the village girls screams **(04:34)** that Turiddu has been killed.

TURIDDU
Mamma, quel vino è generoso, e certo
Oggi troppi bicchier ne ho tracannati...
Vado fuori all'aperto...
Ma prima voglio che mi benedite
Come quel giorno che partii soldato;
E poi, mamma, sentite,
S'io non tornassi voi dovrete fare
Da madre a Santa, ch'io le avea giurato
Di condurla all'altare.

MAMMA LUCIA
Perché parli così, figliuolo mio?

TURIDDU
Oh! Nulla! È il vino che m'ha suggerito!

Per me pregate Iddio!
Un bacio, mamma, un altro bacio, addio;
S'io non tornassi fate da madre a Santa;
Un bacio, mamma, addio!

TURIDDU
Mamma, that is a heady wine: today, I know, I have drunk too many glasses of it... I'll go for some fresh air...But first, before I go, I want you to bless me the way you did that day when I went off to be a soldier; and then, Mamma, listen to me, if I do not return I want you to become a mother to Santa, for I had sworn to lead her to the altar.

MAMMA LUCIA
My son, why are you talking so?

TURIDDU
Oh! It's nothing! It is the wine that's talking!
Pray for me to the Lord!
A kiss, Mamma, another kiss. Goodbye.
If I do not return, you must be a mother to Santa. A kiss, Mamma, goodbye!

(He embraces her and rushes out.)

MAMMA LUCIA

MAMMA LUCIA

(in desperation, running after him)

Oh, Turiddu! Che vuoi dire?

Oh, Turiddu! What are you trying to tell me?

(Santuzza enters.)

Santuzza!

Santuzza!

SANTUZZA

SANTUZZA

(throwing her arms around Mamma Lucia's neck.)

Oh, madre mia!

Oh, my mother!

(A murmur of voices is heard in the distance.)

UNA DONNA *(correndo dal fondo)*
Hanno ammazzato compare Turiddu!
Hanno ammazzato compare Turiddu!

A WOMAN *(running into the square)*
They've killed Turiddu!
They've killed Turiddu!

(The crowd cries out in horror.)

END

FINE

Pagliacci

Act One

PROLOGUE *(Tonio appears through the curtain, dressed as Taddeo in the style of the commedia dell'arte.)*

disc 2/track 1 *Si può? Si può?* An air of expectation springs from the frisky, animated figure the orchestra plays, until **(00:23)** the mood is literally shattered with a sense of uncertainty. A pregnant note in the French horn **(00:44)** leads to a pitiful melody that will reappear in Canio's great aria, followed by a second, more diffident melody **(01:12)** that reappears throughout the opera in relation to Nedda. The uncertainty returns **(01:42)**, followed by echoes of the bustling opening that leads directly into the sudden appearance of Tonio **(02:31)**. He introduces himself, with apologies, deftly explaining why the author has decided on a prologue. The music turns more serious **(04:34)** as he sets the stage for the dreadful story that is about to unfold. But, with broad new melody, Tonio implores the audience to have sympathy for the players of the drama **(05:52)**. With a ringing cry of "On with the show!" **(07:10)**, he bids the players to begin.

TONIO
Si può? Si può?
Signore! Signori! Scusatemi
Se da sol mi presento. Io sono il Prologo.

TONIO
Please? Will you allow me?
Ladies! Gentlemen! Excuse me
if I appear thus alone. I am the Prologue.

99

Poiché in iscena ancor
Le antiche maschere mette l'autore,
In parte ei vuol riprendere
Le vecchie usanze, e a voi
Di nuovo inviami.
Ma non per dirvi come pria
"Le lacrime che noi versiam son false!
Degli spasimi e dei nostri martir
Non allarmatevi!" No. No.
L'autore ha cercato invece pingervi
Uno squarcio di vita.
Egli ha per massima sol che l'artista
È un uom, e che per gli uomini
Scrivere ei deve. Ed al vero ispiravasi.
Un nido di memorie in fondo all'anima
Cantava un giorno, ed ei con vere lacrime
Scrisse, e i singhiozzi il tempo gli batte-
vano!
Dunque, vedrete amar sì come s'amano
Gli esseri umani, vedrete dell'odio
I tristi frutti. Del dolor gli spasimi,
Urli di rabbia, udrete, e risa ciniche!
E voi, piuttosto che le nostre povere
Gabbane d'istrioni, le nostr'anime
Considerate, poiché siam uomini
Di carne e d'ossa, e che di quest'orfano
Mondo al pari di voi spiriamo l'aere!
Il concetto vi dissi. Or ascoltate
Com'egli è svolto.

Since our author is reviving on our stage
the masks of ancient comedy,
he wishes to restore for you, in part,
the old stage customs, and once more
he sends me to you.
But not, as in the past, to reassure you,
saying, "The tears we shed are false,
so do not be alarmed by our agonies
or violence!" No! No!
Our author has endeavoured, rather,
to paint for you a slice of life,
his only maxim being that the artist is a
man, and he must write for men. Truth is
his inspiration.
Deep-embedded memories stirred one day
within his heart, and with real tears
he wrote, and marked the time with sighs!
Now, then, you will see men love
as in real life they love, and you will see
true hatred and its bitter fruit. And you
will hear shouts both of rage and grief, and
cynical laughter.
Mark well, therefore, our souls,
rather than the poor players' garb
we wear, for we are men of flesh and bone,
like you, breathing the same air of this
orphan world.
This, then, is our design. Now give heed
to its unfolding.

(shouting towards the stage)

Andiam. Incominciate!

On with the show! Begin!

A country cross-roads at the entrance to a village.

SCENE ONE

(The blare of trumpet out of tune and the beating of a big drum announce the coming of the players, amid shouts, laughter and the whistling of urchins. A throng of villagers, men and women in holiday dress, come running to the scene. Tonio, annoyed by the swelling crowd, stretchesout in front of the theatre. It is three o'clock under aburning August sun.)

UOMINI E DONNE
(arrivando poco a poco)
Son qua! Ritornano. Pagliaccio è là.
Tutti lo seguono, grandi e ragazzi
E ognun applaude ai motti, ai lazzi.
Ed egli serio saluta e passa
E torna a battere sulla gran cassa.
Ehi! Ehi! Sferza l'asino, bravo Arlecchino!
Son qua! Son qua!
Già fra le strida i monelli
In aria gittano i cappelli!

MEN AND WOMEN
(arriving in groups)
They're here! They're back! And there's
Pagliaccio!
All follow him, young and old,
and all applaud his quips and clowning.
And he bows gravely as he passes,
then beats the big drum again.
Hey! Hey! Whip your donkey, good
Harlequin! They're here, they're here!
Now the urchins shout and throw their
caps in the air!

CANIO *(di dentro)*
Itene al diavolo!

CANIO *(from within)*
Go to the devil!

BEPPE *(di dentro)*
To! To! Birichino!

BEPPE *(from within)*
Take that, you rascal!

CORO
In aria gittano i lor cappelli diggià.
Fra strida e sibili diggià...
Ecco il carretto! Indietro...
Arrivano! Che diavoleria! Dio benedetto!
Arrivano! Indietro! sdraiata

CHORUS
They throw their caps up into the air!
Up they go, with shouts and whistles...
Here come the cart! Make way...
They're coming! Good God, what pande-
monium! They're here...make way!

(Enter Beppe, dressed as Harlequin. He leads a donkey which is drawing a brightly painted, multi-coloured cart. Nedda is reclining in the front of the cart while Canio, in the costume of Pagliaccio, is standing in the back. Canio is beating the big drum.)

TUTTI
Evviva! il principe
Sei de' Pagliacci.
Tu i guai discacci
Col lieto umor.
Evviva! Son qua! ecc.

CANIO
Grazie...

CORO
Bravo!

CANIO
Vorrei...

CORO
E lo spettacolo?

CANIO
Signori miei!

TUTTI
Uh! Ci assorda! Finiscila.

CANIO
Mi accordan di parlar?

TUTTI
Oh! Con lui si dee cedere,
Tacere ed ascoltar.

CANIO
Un grande spettacolo
A ventitré ore

ALL
Hurrah! Hurrah for the
Prince of Clowns!
All cares take flight
before his merriment.
Hurrah! They're here! etc.

CANIO
Thank you...

CHORUS
Bravo!

CANIO
I should like...

CHORUS
And the show?

CANIO
My friends!

ALL
Oh! You deafen us! Stop!

CANIO
Am I allowed to speak?

ALL
Oh! With him we have no choice
but to yield and listen.

CANIO
Your able and respectful
servant is preparing

Prepara il vostr'umile
E buon servitore.
Vedrete le smanie
Del bravo Pagliaccio;
E come ei si vendica
E tende un bel laccio.
Vedrete di Tonio
Tremar la carcassa,
E quale matassa
D'intrighi ordirà.
Venite, onorateci
Signori e Signore.
A ventitré ore!

TUTTI
Verremo, e tu serbaci
Il tuo buon umore.
A ventitré ore!

a great show for you
at eleven this evening.
You will see the madness
of the good Pagliaccio,
and how with a well-laid trap
he gains his vengeance.
You'll see the vile body
of Tonio tremble,
and what a heap of intrigue
that rogue contrives.
Come and honour us,
ladies and gentlemen.
At eleven tonight!

ALL
We'll be there - and save
your good spirits for us!
At eleven tonight!

(Tonio steps forward to help Nedda down from the cart, but Canio, who has already leapt down, gives him a cuff, saying:)

CANIO
Via di lì.

DONNE *(ridendo)*
Prendi questo, bel galante!

RAGAZZI *(fischiando)*
Con salute!

TONIO *(fra sé)*
La pagherai! Brigante.

CANIO
Off with you!

WOMEN *(laughing)*
Take that, you fine gallant!

BOYS *(whistling)*
With our compliments!

TONIO *(to himself)*
You'll pay for this! Bandit!

CANIO

CONTADINO (*a Canio*)
Di', con noi vuoi bevere
Un buon bicchiere sulla crocevia?
Di', vuoi tu?

CANIO
Con piacere.

BEPPE
Aspettatemi,
Anch'io ci sto!

CANIO
Di' Tonio, vieni via?

TONIO
Io netto il somarello. Precedetemi.

CONTADINO (*ridendo*)
Bada, Pagliaccio, ei solo vuol restare
Per far la corte a Nedda.

CANIO (*ghignando, ma con cipiglio*)
Eh! Eh! Vi pare?

(*half serious, half ironic*)

Un tal gioco, credetemi,
È meglio non giocarlo con me, miei cari;
E a Tonio, e un poco a tutti or parlo:
Il teatro e la vita non son la stessa cosa,
E se lassù Pagliaccio Sorprende la sua sposa
Col bel galante in camera,
Fa un comico sermone,
Poi si calma ed arrendesi
Ai colpi di bastone!
Ed il pubblico applaude, ridendo allegra-

VILLAGER (*to Canio*)
Say, won't you come and drink
a glass with us at the cross-roads?
Come, won't you?

CANIO
With pleasure.

BEPPE
Wait for me,
I'll be with you!

CANIO
And you, Tonio, are you coming?

TONIO
I'll groom the donkey. You go ahead.

VILLAGER (*laughing*)
Watch out, Pagliaccio, he wants to be alone
to woo your Nedda.

CANIO (*smiling, but with a frown*)
Ah, so! You think so?

My friends, believe me, it's better
not to play such games with me;
I say to Tonio, and in part to all of you
I say, the stage is one thing and life itself
another; and if up there Pagliaccio
surprises his wife with a lover
in her chamber, why, he delivers a comic
lecture and thereupon calms down
and submits to a thrashing -
and the public applauds to see such sport!

mente. Ma se Nedda sul serio sorprendessi,
Altramente finirebbe la storia,
Com'è ver che vi parlo.
Un tal gioco, credetemi,
È meglio non giocarlo.

NEDDA (*fra sé*)
Confusa io son!

CONTADINI
Sul serio
Pigli dunque la cosa?

CANIO
Io. Vi pare! Scusatemi,
Adoro la mia sposa!

(the sound of bag-pipes off-stage)

RAGAZZI
I zampognari! I zampognari!

UOMINI
Verso la chiesa vanno i compari.

(The church-bells sound vespers.)

I VECCHI
Essi accompagnano la comitiva
Che a coppie al vespero sen va giuliva.

DONNE
Andiam. La campana
Ci appella al Signore.

CANIO
Ma poi ricordatevi
A ventitré ore.

But if I surprised Nedda in real life -
as sure as I am speaking to you -
the story would have a different ending.
It's better not to play
such games, believe me.

NEDDA (*to herself*)
He bewilders me!

VILLAGERS
You take us seriously, then?

CANIO
I! Hardly! Forgive me,
I adore my wife!

BOYS
The pipers! The pipers!

MEN
They are on their way to church.

OLD PEOPLE
They are accompanying the happy train
of couples as they go to vespers.

WOMEN
Come, everyone. The bell
calls us to the Lord.

CANIO
But be sure to remember,
at eleven tonight.

CORO

Andiam, andiam!
Din, don. Suona vespero,
Ragazze e garzon,
A coppie al tempio affrettiamoci
C'affrettiam! Din, don!
Diggià i culmini,
Din, don, vuol baciar.
Le mamme ci adocchiano,
Attenti, compar.
Din, don. Tutto irradiasi
Di luce e d'amor.
Ma i vecchi sorvegliano
Gli arditi amador.
Din, don. ecc.

CHORUS

Let's go, let's go!
Ring, bells! It is vespers calling,
girls and lads, let us join
in pairs and hasten now
to church. Ring, bells!
Yonder the sun kisses
the western heights, ring, bells!
Look out, companions,
our mothers watch us.
Ring, bells! The world is gleaming
with light and love.
But our elders keep watch
over bold lovers!
Ring, bells! etc.

SCENE TWO

(During the chorus, Canio has gone behind the theatre to take off his Pagliaccio costume. He returns, nods a smiling farewell to Nedda and leaves with Beppe and five or six villagers. Nedda remains alone.)

disc no. 2/track 6 *Qual fiamma avea nel guardo!...Hui! Stridono lassù* Nedda worries about the glint of jealousy she has just seen in Canio's eyes and what it might portend. The orchestra banishes the air of concern by into glowing, gentle chords as he raises her face to the midsummer sun **(01:00)** and lets its warmth calm her. When she opens her eyes, Nedda is delighted by the flight of birds she sees in the sky **(02:01)**. The chirping of the flutes over the high strings **(02:43)** introduces the graceful Ballatella she sings, marveling at (and yearning for) the limitless freedom of the birds in the sky.

NEDDA

Qual fiamma avea nel guardo.
Gli occhi abbassai per tema ch'ei leggesse
Il mio pensier segreto.

NEDDA

What a fire in his glance!
I lowered my eyes for fear that he read my
secret thoughts. Oh, if he ever caught me,

Oh! S'ei mi sorprendesse,
Brutale come egli è. Ma basti, orvia.
Son questi sogni paurosi e fole!
O che bel sole di mezz'agosto!
Io son piena di vita, e, tutta illanguidita
Per arcano desìo, non so che bramo!

(She looks up at the sky.)

Oh! Che volo d'augelli, e quante strida!
Che chiedon? Dove van?
Chissà? La mamma mia, che la buona ven-
tura Annunciava, comprendeva il lor canto
E a me bambina così cantava:
Hui! Stridono lassù, liberamente
Lanciati a vol come frecce, gli augel.
Disfidano le nubi e il sol cocente,
E vanno, e vanno per le vie del ciel.
Lasciateli vagar per l'atmosfera
Questi assetati di azzurro e di splendor;
Seguono anch'essi un sogno, una chimera,
E vanno, e vanno fra le nubi d'or.
Che incalzi il vento e latri la tempesta,
Con l'ali aperte san tutto sfidar;
La pioggia, i lampi, nulla mai li arresta,
E vanno, e vanno sugli abissi e i mar.
Vanno laggiù verso un paese strano
Che sognan forse e che cercano invan.
Ma i boëmi del ciel seguon l'arcano
Poter che li sospinge, e van, e van!

(Tonio enters during the song and listens enchanted. Nedda sees him as she finishes.)

Sei là! Credea che te ne fossi andato.

brute that he is! But enough of that.
These are mere fearful dreams and folly.
Oh, beautiful midsummer sun!
And I, bursting with life, languid with
desire, and yet not knowing what it is I
long for!

Oh, what a flight of birds, what clamour!
What do they seek? Where do they go?
Who knows?... My mother, who foretold
the future, understood their song and even
so she sang to me as a child.
Hui! How wildly they shout up there,
launched on their flight like arrows!
They defy storm-clouds and burning sun,
as they fly on and on through the heaven.
Light-thirsty ones, avid for air and
splendour, let them pursue their journey;
they, too, follow a dream and a chimera,
journeying on and on through clouds of
gold. Let winds buffet and storms toss
them, they challenge all with open wings;
neither rain nor lightning daunts them,
neither sea nor chasms, as they fly on and
on. They journey towards a strange land
yonder, a land they've dreamt of, which
they seek in vain... Vagabonds of the sky,
who obey only the secret force that drives
them on and on.

You here! I thought you'd gone!

TONIO
È colpa del tuo canto.
Affascinato io mi beava!

NEDDA
Ah! ah! Quanta poesia!

TONIO
Non rider, Nedda.

NEDDA
Va, va all'osteria.

TONIO
So ben che lo scemo contorto son io;
Che desto soltanto lo scherno e l'orror.
Eppure ha 'l pensiero un sogno, un desìo,
E un palpito il cor!
Allor che sdegnosa mi passi d'accanto,
Non sai tu che pianto mi spreme il dolor,
Perché, mio malgrado, subito ho l'incanto,
M'ha vinto l'amor!
Oh, lasciami, lasciami or dirti...

NEDDA
Che m'ami?
Hai tempo a ridirmelo
Stasera, se il brami
Facendo le smorfie Colà sulla scena.

TONIO
Non rider, Nedda.

NEDDA
Tal pena puoi risparmiar!

TONIO
Only your singing is to blame.
I listened enraptured.

NEDDA
Ah, such a fine speech!

TONIO
Don't laugh at me, Nedda...

NEDDA
Off with you...off to the tavern.

TONIO
I know well that I am the twisted half-wit,
that I inspire only scorn and loathing.
But even so, I too dream dreams; I too
know in my heart the pulsing of desire.
When you pass coldly by me, in disdain,
you do not know what anguish grips me...
For I have felt the sorcery, alas, and
I am vanquished in your spell.
Oh, let me speak and tell you...

NEDDA
That you love me?
You will have time to tell me that
tonight, if you so wish, while you perform
your tricks there on the stage.

TONIO
Don't laugh at me, Nedda.

NEDDA
But now please spare yourself the trouble.

TONIO
No, è qui che voglio dirtelo,
E tu m'ascolterai,
Che t'amo e ti desidero,
E che tu mia sarai!

NEDDA
Eh! Dite, mastro Tonio!
La schiena oggi vi prude, o una tirata
D'orecchi è necessaria Al vostro ardor?

TONIO
Ti beffi? Sciagurata?
Per la croce di Dio, bada che puoi
Pagarla cara!

NEDDA
Tu minacci? Vuoi
Che vada a chiamar Canio?

TONIO
Non prima ch'io ti baci.

NEDDA
Oh, bada!

TONIO

(advancing with open arms to seize her)

Oh, tosto sarai mia!

NEDDA

(seizes Beppe's whip and lashes Tonio across the face.)

TONIO
No, here and now I want to tell you,
and you shall hear me say,
that I adore you and desire you and that
you will be mine!

NEDDA
Eh! Tell me, Master Tonio!
Have you an itching back, or must I
pull your ears to cool your ardour?

TONIO
You mock me? Wretched woman!
By God's Cross, watch out or you'll
pay dearly for it!

NEDDA
You're threatening me?
Shall I call Canio?

TONIO
Not until I kiss you.

NEDDA
Look out!

TONIO

Oh, you will soon be mine!

NEDDA

Miserabile!

TONIO (*dà un urlo e retrocede*)
Per la Vergin pia di mezz'agosto
Nedda, lo giuro, me la pagherai!

(He goes out, growling threats.)

NEDDA
Aspide! Va. Ti sei svelato ormai!
Tonio lo scemo.
Hai l'animo Siccome il corpo tuo difforme,
lurido!

(Enter Silvio, who calls softly.)

SILVIO
Nedda!

NEDDA
Silvio! A quest'ora che imprudenza.

SILVIO
Ah, bah! Sapea ch'io non rischiavo nulla.
Canio e Beppe da lunge alla taverna
Ho scorto! Ma prudente
Per la macchia a me nota qui ne venni.

NEDDA
E ancora un poco in Tonio t'imbattevi.

Wretch!

TONIO (*falling back with a scream*)
By the Holy Virgin of the Assumption,
Nedda, I swear, you'll pay for this!

NEDDA
Snake that you are, go! Now that you have
shown what you are! Tonio the half-wit!
Your soul is like your body, filthy and
deformed!

SILVIO
Nedda!

NEDDA
Silvio! How rash at this hour!

SILVIO
Bah! I knew I was risking nothing.
I saw both Canio and Beppe far off
at the tavern, and I came here cautiously
through woods I know.

NEDDA
A moment earlier and you'd have met
Tonio!

SILVIO
Oh! Tonio lo scemo!

NEDDA
Lo scemo è da temersi.
M'ama. Or qui mel disse, e nel bestiale
Delirio suo, baci chiedendo,
Ardiva correr su me.

SILVIO
Per Dio!

NEDDA
Ma con la frusta
Del cane immondo la foga calmai.

SILVIO
E fra quest'ansie in eterno vivrai;
Nedda, Nedda,
Decidi il mio destin,
Nedda, Nedda rimani!
Tu il sai, la festa ha fin E parte ognun
domani. Nedda, Nedda!
E quando tu di qui sarai partita
Che addiverrà di me, della mia vita?

NEDDA
Silvio!

SILVIO
Nedda, Nedda, rispondimi.
Se è ver che Canio non amasti mai,
Se è vero che t'è in odio
Il ramingare e il mestier che tu fai,
Se l'immenso amor tuo una fola non è,
Questa notte partiam! Fuggi, fuggi, con
me.

SILVIO
Oh, Tonio the half-wit!

NEDDA
The half-wit is to be feared!
He loves me - so he told me now - and in
his bestial passion dared assault me,
yelling for kisses.

SILVIO
By God!

NEDDA
But with the whip
I curbed the fury of the filthy dog!

SILVIO
Ah, you will live forever with this worry...
Oh, Nedda, Nedda,
resolve my fate, stay with me, Nedda, stay!
You know the holiday is ending
and everyone will leave tomorrow.
Nedda, Nedda!
What will become of me and of my life
when you have gone away?

NEDDA
Silvio!

SILVIO
Nedda, Nedda, answer me.
If it is true that you have never loved
Canio, if, as you say, you loathe
this wandering life and trade,
and if your great love for me is not a myth,
come, let us flee tonight! Come, flee with
me!

NEDDA

Non mi tentar! Vuoi tu perder la mia vita?
Taci, Silvio, non più. È deliro, è follia!
Io mi confido a te cui diedi il cor.
Non abusar di me, del mio febbrile amor!
Non mi tentar! Pietà di me!
Non mi tentar! E poi chissà! meglio è par-
tir.
Sta il destin contro noi, è vano il nostro
dir!
Eppure dal mio cor strapparti non poss'io,
Vivrò sol dell'amor ch'hai destato al cor
mio!

SILVIO

Ah! Nedda! fuggiam!

NEDDA

Non mi tentar! Vuoi tu perder la vita mia?
ecc.

SILVIO

Nedda, rimani!
Che mai sarà di me quando sarai partita?
Riman! Nedda! Fuggiam! Deh vien!
Ah! fuggi con me!
Deh vien!
No, più non m'ami!

TONIO (scorgendoli, a parte)
T'ho colta, sgualdrina!

NEDDA

Sì, t'amo, t'amo!

NEDDA

Oh, do not tempt me! would you ruin my
life?
Quiet, Silvio, quiet. This is madness!
I put my trust in you, who have my heart...
Do not abuse my ardent passion!
Do not tempt me! Take pity on me!
Do not tempt me! And then who knows?
It's best to part.
Fate is against us, our words are in vain!
Yet from my heart I cannot tear you. I shall
live only on the love which you awakened
in my heart!

SILVIO

Oh! Nedda, let us flee!

NEDDA

Do not tempt me! Would you ruin my life?
etc.

SILVIO

Nedda, stay!
What will happen to me when you've
gone?
Stay! Nedda! Let's fly! Ah, come!
Ah! Come with me! Ah, come!
No! You love me no longer!

TONIO (observing them from one side)
Wench, I've caught you now!

NEDDA

Yes, I love you, I love you!

SILVIO

E parti domattina?
E allor perché, di', tu m'hai stregato
Se vuoi lasciarmi senza pietà?
Quel bacio tuo perché me l'hai dato
Fra spasmi ardenti di voluttà?
Se tu scordasti l'ore fugaci
Io non lo posso, e voglio ancor
Que' spasmi ardenti, que' caldi baci
Che tanta febbre m'han messo in cor!

NEDDA

Nulla scordai, sconvolta e turbata m'ha
Questo amor che nel guardo ti sfavilla.
Viver voglio a te avvinta, affascinata,
Una vita d'amor calma e tranquilla.
A te mi dono; su me solo impera.
Ed io ti prendo e m'abbandono intera.

NEDDA E SILVIO

Tutto scordiam.

NEDDA

Negli occhi mi guarda! mi guarda!
Baciami, baciami! Tutto scordiamo!

SILVIO

Verrai?

NEDDA

Sì. Baciami.

SILVIO

And you will leave tomorrow?
Why, if you must leave me without pity,
why then, sorceress, have you ensnared me?
Why then, that kiss of yours in the abandon of your close embrace?
If you forget those fleeting hours,
I cannot do so: I desire still that warm
abandon and that flaming kiss
that kindled such a fire in my blood!

NEDDA

I have forgotten nothing: I have been
stirred and shaken by your burning love.
All I wish is to share a life of love with you,
bound to you ever in a sweet enchantment.
To you I give myself and you I take;
you alone rule me: I am wholly yours.

NEDDA AND SILVIO

Let us forget everything.

NEDDA

Look into my eyes! Loot at me!
Kiss me, kiss me! Let us forget everything!

SILVIO

You will come?

NEDDA

Yes. Kiss me.

NEDDA E SILVIO
Sì, ti guardo e ti bacio;
t'amo, t'amo!

NEDDA AND SILVIO
Yes, I look at you, I kiss you,
I love you, I love you!

(Canio and Tonio come furtively in as Nedda and Silvio are approaching the wall.)

TONIO
Cammina adagio e li sorprenderai.

TONIO
Walk softly and you'll surprise them.

SILVIO
Ad alta notte laggiù mi terrò.
Cauta discendi e mi ritroverai.

SILVIO
I'll be down there at midnight.
Come cautiously and you will find me.

(Silvio vaults over the wall.)

NEDDA
A stanotte, e per sempre tua sarò!

NEDDA
Until tonight, and I'll be yours forever.

CANIO
Oh!

CANIO
Oh!

NEDDA
Fuggi

NEDDA
Run!

(Canio also scales the wall in pursuit of Silvio.)

Aiutalo, Signor!

Heaven help him!

CANIO *(fuori scena)*
Vile, t'ascondi!

CANIO *(off-stage)*
You're hiding, coward!

TONIO *(ridendo cinicamente)*
Ah!...Ah!...

TONIO *(laughing cynically)*
Ha!...Ha!...

NEDDA
Bravo! Bravo il mio Tonio!

NEDDA
Bravo! Bravo, Master Tonio!

TONIO
Fo quello che posso!

NEDDA
È quello che pensavo!

TONIO
Ma di far assai meglio non dispero.

NEDDA
Mi far schifo e ribrezzo.

TONIO
Oh, non sai come
Lieto ne son!

(Canio returns, wiping his brow.)

CANIO *(con rabbia)*
Derisione e scherno!
Nulla! Ei ben lo conosce quel sentier.
Fa lo stesso; poiché del drudo il nome
Or mi dirai.

NEDDA
Chi?

CANIO *(furente)*
Tu, pel Padre Eterno!

(drawing a stiletto from his belt)

E se in questo momento qui scannata
Non t'ho, già, gli è perché pria di lordarla
Nel tuo fetido sangue, o svergognata,
Codesta lama, io vo' il suo nome. Parla!

TONIO
I do what I can.

NEDDA
That's as I thought!

TONIO
But I have not lost hope of doing better.

NEDDA
You fill me with disgust and loathing!

TONIO
Oh, you don't know
how glad that makes me!

CANIO *(raging)*
Scorn and derision!
Empty-handed! He knows that path well.
But no matter! For you yourself will tell me
now the scoundrel's name.

NEDDA
Who?

CANIO *(furious)*
You, by the Almighty!

And if I have not cut your throat
already at this moment, it's because
I want his name before this blade
is fouled with your stinking blood. Speak!

NEDDA
Vano è l'insulto.
È muto il labbro mio.

CANIO
Il nome, il nome, non tardare,
o donna!

NEDDA
Non lo dirò giammai.

CANIO

(rushing at her in a fury with stiletto raised)

Per la Madonna!

(Beppe enters and wrests the knife from Canio.)

BEPPE
Padron! Che fate! Per l'amor di Dio.
La gente esce di chiesa e allo spettacolo
Qui muove; andiamo, via, calmatevi!

CANIO *(dibattendosi)*
Lasciami, Beppe. Il nome, il nome!

BEPPE
Tonio, Vieni a tenerlo. Andiamo, arriva il
pubblico.

(Tonio takes Canio by the hand and Beppe turns to Nedda.)

Vi spiegherete. E voi di lì tiratevi,
Andatevi a vestir. Sapete, Canio
È violento, ma buono.

NEDDA
It is no use insulting me. My lips are
sealed.

CANIO
His name, his name! Don't waste time,
woman!

NEDDA
I'll never tell you.

CANIO

By the Madonna!

BEPPE
Master! What are you doing? By God's
love, the villagers are leaving church and
coming to the show. Come, calm down!

CANIO *(struggling)*
Let go, Beppe! His name! His name!

BEPPE
Tonio, come here and hold him. Hurry, the
public is arriving.

You'll do your explaining later. You there,
get going. Go and get dressed. You know,
Canio is hot-tempered but good-hearted.

(He pushes Nedda through the curtain and follows her.)

CANIO
Infamia! Infamia!

CANIO
Shameful! Shameful!

TONIO
Calmatevi, padrone. È meglio fingere;
Il ganzo tornerà. Di me fidatevi.
Io la sorveglio. Ora facciam la recita.
Chissà ch'egli non venga allo spettacolo
E si tradisca!
Or via! Bisogna fingere
Per riuscir.

TONIO
Be calm now, Master, it is better to
dissemble.
The lover will be back. Trust me,
I'll keep an eye on her. Now for the show!
Who knows, perhaps he'll come to see the
play and so betray himself. To succeed
you must dissemble.

BEPPE *(Rientra.)*
Andiamo, via, vestitevi,
Padrone. E tu batti la cassa, Tonio.

BEPPE *(re-entering)*
Come one, Master, hurry,
you must dress. And you, Tonio, beat the
drum.

(Tonio and Beppe leave. Canio, overwhelmed, remains behind.)

disc no. 2
tracks 14 & 15

Recitar!..Mentre preso dal delirio...Vesti la giubba Rough, stuttering
chords **(Track 14)** introduce Canio's anguished monologue, in which his psychotic
self-pity emerges, when he bitterly laughs **(00:33)** at his own assertion that he
is not a man. Almost in a daze **(Track 15)**, he begins to put on his makeup
and costume. The uneasy vocal line suggests his stupor as he imagines himself
as the cuckolded Pagliaccio in the play he is about to perform. His anguish
explodes **(01:01)**—in one of the most famous cries in all of opera—as he bitterly
describes Pagliaccio laughing at his predicament.

CANIO
Recitar! Mentre preso dal delirio
Non so più quel che dico e quel che faccio!
Eppur...è d'uopo...sforzati!
Bah, se' tu forse un uom!

CANIO
Perform the play! While I am racked with
grief, not knowing what I say or what I do!
And yet...I must...ah, force myself to do it!
Bah! You are not a man!

Tu se' Pagliaccio!	You are Pagliaccio!
Vesti la giubba e la faccia infarina.	Put on the costume, the powder and the
La gente paga e rider vuole qua.	paint: the people pay and want to laugh.
E se Arlecchin t'invola Colombina,	And if Harlequin steals your Columbine,
Ridi Pagliaccio, e ognun applaudirà!	laugh, Pagliaccio, and all will applaud you!
Tramuta in lazzi lo spasmo ed il pianto;	Change all your tears and anguish into
In una smorfia il singhiozzo e il dolore...	clowning:
Ridi Pagliaccio, sul tuo amore infranto!	and into a grimace your sobbing and your
Ridi del duol che t'avvelena il cor!	pain... Laugh, Pagliaccio, at your shattered
	love! Laugh at the sorrow that has rent
	your heart!

Act 2

(Grief-stricken, he goes out through the curtain.)

disk no. 2/track 16 *Intermezzo* The orchestra echoes the sense of stark desolation in Canio's soul before seguing into a passionate restatement of the soulful melody heard in Tonio's prologue **(00:59)**. But the music suddenly spins out of control **(01:28)**, with violins shrieking out the musical figure that accompanied Canio's cries of "Laugh, clown, life." When they recede and calm is restored, the melody from the prologue returns **(01:47)**, stronger this time and heavy with sorrow, finishing passionately, undercut with echoes in the basses of Canio's cries.

(All members of the troupe are on stage. The spectators arrive in groups.)

LE DONNE	**WOMEN**
Presto, affrettiamoci,	Come on, friend,
Svelto, compare. Ché lo spettacolo Dee	quick, keep moving,

cominciare. Cerchiam di metterci
Ben sul davanti.

TONIO
Si dà principio,
Avanti, avanti!

GLI UOMINI
Veh, come corrono
Le bricconcelle!
Accomodatevi,
Comari belle.
O Dio che correre
Per giunger tosto qua!

TONIO
Pigliate posto!

CORO
Cerchiamo posto!
Ben sul davanti!
Cerchiam di metterci
Ben sul davanti,
Ché lo spettacolo
Dee cominciare.

TONIO
Avanti!
Pigliate posto, su!

LE DONNE
Ma non pigiatevi,
Pigliate posto!
Su, Beppe, aiutaci.
V'è posto accanto!

the show is starting at any minute.
Let's try to sit right at the front.

TONIO
We're about to start!
Your seats, everyone!

THE MEN
See how the ladies run,
the little rascals!
Fair friends,
please be seated.
Good heavens, what a crush
to get in first.

TONIO
Take your places!

CHORUS
Let's find a place!
Right at the front!
Let's try to sit
right at the front,
for the show
is about to begin.

TONIO
Come on!
Take your seats, please!

THE WOMEN
Don't push and crowd,
take your places!
Come, Beppe, help us,
there's a place right here!

UNA PARTE DEL CORO
Suvvia, spicciatevi,
ncominciate.
Perché tardate?
Siam tutti là.

BEPPE
Che furia, diavolo!
Prima pagate.
Nedda, incassate.

UN'ALTRA PARTE DEL CORO
Veh, si accapigliano!
Chiamano aiuto!
Ma via, sedetevi
Senza gridar.

SILVIO
Nedda!

NEDDA
Sii cauto!
Non t'ha veduto.

SILVIO
Verrò ad attenderti.
Non obliar!

CORO
Di qua! Di qua!
Incominciate!
Perché tardar!
Suvvia questa commedia!
Facciam rumore!
Diggià suonar ventitré ore!
Allo spettacolo ognun anela! Ah!

PART OF THE CHORUS
On with the show!
Come on, let's get started!
Why the waiting?
We're all here!

BEPPE
The devil, what a racket!
You've got to pay first!
Nedda, take the money.

ANOTHER PART OF THE CHORUS
Look, they're fighting,
calling for help!
Quiet there, sit down
and stop shouting.

SILVIO
Nedda!

NEDDA
Careful!
He didn't see you!

SILVIO
I'll be waiting for you!
Don't forget!

CHORUS
This way! This way!
Start the show!
Why the delay?
Get on with the play!
Let's make a row!
Eleven o'clock has struck!
Everyone longs to see the show! Ah!

S'alza la tela!
Silenzio. Olà.

The curtain's rising!
Quiet! Holà!

THE PLAY

Nedda (Columbine) - Beppe (Harlequin)
Canio (Pagliaccio) - Tonio (Taddeo)

(The curtain of the inner stage rises, disclosing a little room with a table and two chairs. Nedda, in costume of Columbine, is pacing anxiously up and down.)

disk 2/track 19

Oh! Colombina A brief but disarmingly beautiful moment in the score— a gentle little serenade to Colombina, sung by Arlecchino (played by Beppe, a member of the troupe) over pizzicato (plucked) strings. This serenade is a favorite of lyric tenors, whose voices are too light to sing the demanding role of Canio.

NEDDA *(Colombina)*
Pagliaccio, mio marito,
A tarda notte sol ritornerà.
E quello scimunito di Taddeo
Perché mai non è ancor qui?

LA VOCE DI BEPPE *(Arlecchino)*
Ah! Colombina, il tenero
Fido Arlecchin
È a te vicin!
Di te chiamando,
E sospirando, aspetta il poverin!
La tua faccetta mostrami,
Ch'io vo' baciar Senza tardar La tua boc-cuccia. Amor mi cruccia e mi sta a tormen-tar! Ah! Colombina schiudimi

NEDDA *(Columbine)*
My husband Pagliaccio
will not be home till late.
And whatever has become
of that blockhead Taddeo?

THE VOICE OF BEPPE *(Harlequin)*
Oh! Columbine, your faithful
and adoring Harlequin
is near!
Calling your name and sighing, the poor
fellow awaits you!
Show your fair face that I may kiss
this instant your little mouth.
Love is cruelly tormenting me!
Oh, Columbine,

Il finestrin, Che a te vicin
Di te chiamando
E sospirando è il povero Arlecchin!
A te vicin è Arlecchin!
NEDDA (Colombina)
Di fare il segno convenuto appressa
L'istante ed Arlecchino aspetta!

open your window for me; your poor,
patient Harlequin is waiting,
sighing and calling your name!
Harlequin is near to you!

NEDDA (Columbine)
Harlequin is waiting, and the hour is near
for the agreed signal!

(Nedda sits at the table, her back towards the door. Enter Tonio, dressed as the servant Taddeo. Unseen by Nedda, he pauses a moment to admire her.)

TONIO (Taddeo)
È dessa! Dei, come è bella!

TONIO (Taddeo)
She herself! Ye gods, how divine!

(The public laughs.)

Se alla rubella
Io disvelassi
L'amor mio che commuove sino i sassi!
Lungi è lo sposo,
Perché non oso?
Soli noi siamo
E senza alcun sospetto!
Orsù. Proviamo!

If I should reveal
my love to this shrew,
this love mightier than mountains!
And why not dare?
Her husband is away!
And we are alone
and unsuspected!
Up, then! Let us try!

(A deep and exaggerated sigh. The public laughs.)

NEDDA (Colombina)
(volgendosi)
Sei tu, bestia?

NEDDA (Columbine)
(turning)
Is it you, you idiot?

TONIO (Taddeo)
Quell'io sono, sì!

TONIO (Taddeo)
My very self.

NEDDA (Colombina)
E Pagliaccio è partito?

NEDDA (Columbine)
And Pagliaccio has gone?

TONIO (*Taddeo*)
Egli partì!

NEDDA (*Colombina*)
Che fai così impalato?
Il pollo hai tu comprato?

TONIO (*Taddeo*)
Ecco, vergin divina!

(*falling to his knees and offering the basket*)

Ed anzi eccoci entrambi ai piedi tuoi,
Poiché l'ora è suonata o Colombina,
Di svelarti il mio cor. Di', udirmi vuoi?
Dal dì...

NEDDA (*Colombina*)

(*grabbing the basket*)

Quanto spendesti dal trattore?

TONIO (*Taddeo*)
Uno e cinquanta. Da quel dì il mio core...

NEDDA (*Colombina*)
Non seccarmi, Taddeo!

(*Harlequin leaps in through the window. He places a bottle on the table, and then goes towards Taddeo, who pretends not to see him.*)

TONIO (*Taddeo*)
So che sei pura
E casta al par di neve!

TONIO (*Taddeo*)
Gone!

NEDDA (*Columbine*)
Why are you standing there transfixed?
Did you buy the chicken?

TONIO (*Taddeo*)
Divine lady, here it is!

And here, indeed, we both lie at your feet,
for the hour has come, O Columbine,
to disclose my whole heart to you. Say,
will you listen? From the day...

NEDDA (*Columbine*)

How much did you pay the inn-keeper?

TONIO (*Taddeo*)
One and a half. From that day my heart...

NEDDA (*Columbine*)
Stop bothering me, Taddeo!

TONIO (*Taddeo*)
I know that you are chaste
and pure as whitest snow!

E ben che dura ti mostri,
Ad obbliarti non riesco!

BEPPE (*Arlecchino*)

(*takes Taddeo by the ear and gives him a kick*)

Va a pigliar il fresco!

(*Spectators laugh.*)

TONIO (*Taddeo*)

(*beating a comic retreat*)

Numi! S'aman! M'arrendo ai detti tuoi.
Vi benedico!
Là, veglio su voi!

(*Exit Taddeo. The public applauds.*)

NEDDA (*Colombina*)
Arlecchin!

BEPPE (*Arlecchino*)
Colombina! Alfin s'arrenda
Ai nostri prieghi amor!

NEDDA (*Colombina*)
Facciam merenda.

(*They sit facing each other at the table.*)

Guarda, amor mio, che splendida
Cenetta preparai!

And harsh as you are towards me,
I cannot forget you!

BEPPE (*Harlequin*)

Go outside and cool off!

TONIO (*Taddeo*)

Heavens! They are in love! I yield to your
orders, and bless you! Now, I'll keep watch
for you!

NEDDA (*Columbine*)
Harlequin!

BEPPE (*Harlequin*)
Columbine! Love at long last
surrenders to our prayers!

NEDDA (*Columbine*)
Let's have a little supper.

See, my love, what a splendid
repast I've made for you!

BEPPE (*Arlecchino*)
Guarda, amor mio, che nettare
Divino t'apportai!

INSIEME
L'amor ama gli effluvii
Del vin, della cucina!

BEPPE (*Arlecchino*)
Mia ghiotta Colombina!

NEDDA (*Colombina*)
Amabile beone!

BEPPE (*Arlecchino*)

(taking out a phial)

Prendi questo narcotico,
Dallo a Pagliaccio pria che s'addormenti,
E poi fuggiam insiem.

NEDDA (*Colombina*)
Sì, porgi.

(Re-enter Taddeo, in an exaggerated fit of trembling.)

TONIO (*Taddeo*)
Attenti!
Pagliaccio è là tutto stravolto, ed armi
Cerca! Ei sa tutto. Io corro a barricarmi!

(He rushes out slamming the door.)

NEDDA (*Colombina*)

BEPPE (*Harlequin*)
See, my love, what a heavenly
nectar I've brought you!

TOGETHER
True love adores
the joys of food and wine!

BEPPE (*Harlequin*)
My greedy Columbine!

NEDDA (*Columbine*)
Beloved drunkard!

BEPPE (*Harlequin*)

Take this drug and give it to Pagliaccio
before he goes to sleep,
and then we'll run off together.

NEDDA (*Columbine*)
Yes, let me have it.

TONIO (*Taddeo*)
Look out!
Pagliaccio's here, raging like a madman,
seeking arms. He knows all. I'll barricade
myself!

NEDDA (*Columbine*)

(to Harlequin)

Via!	Flee!

BEPPE _(Arlecchino)_ | **BEPPE** _(Harlequin)_

(climbing through the window)

Versa il filtro nella tazza sua. | Pour the filter into his cup.

(Enter Canio, dressed as Pagliaccio.)

NEDDA _(Colombina)_
A stanotte, e per sempre io sarò tua.

NEDDA _(Columbine)_
Till tonight, and I shall be yours forever!

CANIO _(Pagliaccio)_
(Nome di Dio! Quelle stesse parole!
Coraggio!) Un uomo era con te.

CANIO _(Pagliaccio)_
(In God's name! The very words!
Courage!) A man was here with you.

NEDDA _(Colombina)_
Che fole!
Sei briaco?

NEDDA _(Columbine)_
What nonsense!
Are you drunk?

CANIO _(Pagliaccio)_
Briaco, sì, da un'ora!

CANIO
(Pagliaccio)
Drunk, yes, for an hour!

NEDDA _(Colombina)_
Tornasti presto.

NEDDA _(Columbine)_
You are home early.

CANIO _(Pagliaccio)_

CANIO _(Pagliaccio)_

(significantly)

Ma in tempo! T'accora,
Dolce sposina?

But in time! Does that
distress you, sweet wife?

(resuming the play)

Ah, sola io ti credea
E due posti son là.

Ah, I thought you were alone...
But I see two places.

NEDDA *(Colombina)*
Con me sedea Taddeo che là si chiuse
Per paura.

NEDDA *(Columbine)*
Taddeo was with me, and scampered off
for fear.

(towards the door)

Orsù, parla!

You, there, speak up!

TONIO *(Taddeo)*
Credetela. Essa è pura!
E aborre dal mentir quel labbro pio!

TONIO *(Taddeo)*
Believe her! She is pure!
Her pious lips abhor all falsehood!

(Spectators laugh loudly.)

CANIO *(rabbiosamente al pubblico)*
Per la morte!

CANIO *(furiously to the public)*
The devil take you!

(then to Nedda)

Smettiamo! Ho dritto anch'io
D'agir come ogni altr'uomo. Il nome suo!

This is enough. I have the right to act
like every other man! His name!

NEDDA *(fredda e sorridente)*
Di chi?

NEDDA *(cold and smiling)*
Whose?

CANIO
Vo il nome dell'amante tuo,
Del drudo infame a cui ti desti in braccio,
O turpe donna!

CANIO
I want your lover's name.
Name me the villain to whom you gave
yourself, base harlot!

NEDDA *(sempre recitando la commedia)*
Pagliaccio! Pagliaccio!

NEDDA *(still acting her part)*
Pagliaccio! Pagliaccio!

No, Pagliaccio non son...Suvvia, così terribile Reality comes crashing down on the commedia plays as Canio angrily announces to one and all that it is no longer Pagliaccio they are watching. The audience is clueless **(01:21)**, so convinced are they by the drama they are witnessing, though Silvio can barely contain his fury. Canio is oblivious to their comments **(01:41)**, launching into a increasingly more ominous tirade against his unfaithful mate. The ignorant audience greets his statement with "Bravo!"s **(03:02)**, though Nedda can see what is going on. Canio's bitter response is greeted with her determination to get the play going again **(Track 24)**. But Canio erupts in a fury **(00:35)**, confronting her directly to name her lover. With a cry of "No!" **(00:59)**, she tries to escape him and the crowd grows uneasy with what they are watching. Silvio draws his dagger but too late—Canio has stabbed her **(01:33)**, and then turns his rage on her lover **(01:59)**. He turns to the horrified audience and numbly announces that the play has ended, as the orchestra thunders in with a repeat of the cries of "Laugh, clown, laugh!" from his aria.

CANIO
No, Pagliaccio non son; se il viso è pallido
È di vergogna e smania di vendetta!
L'uom riprende i suoi dritti, e il cor
Che sanguina vuol sangue a lavar l'onta,
O maledetta! No, Pagliaccio non son!
Son quei che stolido ti raccolse
Orfanella in su la via
Quasi morta di fame, e un nome offriati
Ed un amor ch'era febbre e follia!

DONNE
Comare, mi fa piangere!
Par vera questa scena!

UOMINI
Zitte laggiù!
Che diamine!

CANIO
No, I am not Pagliaccio! Although my face is white, that is for shame and for the lust for vengeance! The man reclaims his right, the heart that bleeds wants blood to wash away the shame, damned woman! No, I am not Pagliaccio! I am he, I am that fool who found you, a starving orphan of the street, and took you in, and offered you a name, and the fever and the folly of his love!

WOMEN
Friend, it makes me weep,
so true the play appears!

MEN
Keep quiet there!
The devil take you!

SILVIO (*fra sé*)
Io mi ritengo appena!

CANIO
Sperai, tanto il delirio
Accecato m'aveva,
Se non amor, pietà, mercè!
Ed ogni sacrifizio Al cor, lieto, imponeva,
E fidente credeva
Più che in Dio stesso, in te!
Ma il vizio alberga sol
Nell'alma tua negletta:
Tu viscere non hai...
Sol legge è 'l senso a te;
Va, non merti il mio duol,
O meretrice abbietta,
Vo' nello sprezzo mio
Schiacciarti sotto i piè!

LA FOLLA
Bravo!

NEDDA (*fredda ma seria*)
Ebben, se mi giudichi
Di te indegna, mi scaccia in questo istante.

CANIO (*sogghignando*)
Ah, ah! Di meglio chiedere
Non dêi che correr tosto al caro amante.
Sei furba! No, per Dio, tu resterai
E 'l nome del tuo ganzo mi dirai.

NEDDA (*cercando di riprendere la commedia*)
Suvvia, così terribile
Davver non ti credea!
Qui nulla v'ha di tragico.

SILVIO (*to himself*)
I can hardly contain myself!

CANIO
So blinded was I by my passion,
that I had hoped - if not for love -
at least for merciful compassion!
And gladly every sacrifice
I placed upon my heart,
and trustful, I believed in you
more than in God Himself!
But only evil dwells
in your abandoned soul:
yes, you are heartless and you know
no law but of your senses.
Go, you do not deserve my grief,
woman without shame!
In my disgust I will
crush you beneath my feet!

THE CROWD
Bravo!

NEDDA (*cold but serious*)
Well, then, if you so judge me
unworthy of you, drive me out forthwith!

CANIO (*with derision*)
Ah, ha! You could ask for nothing better
than to run off to your paramour. You are
cunning! But no, by God, you'll stay
and tell me now your lover's name!

NEDDA (*trying to resume the play*)
Now, there, get going. Truly I never
thought
you could be so terrible.

Vieni a dirgli, o Taddeo,
Che l'uom seduto or dianzi a me vicino
Era il pauroso ed innocuo Arlecchino!

There is no tragic business here.
Taddeo, come now and tell him
that the man sitting with me here a while
ago was our own timorous and harmless
Harlequin!

(She stifles her laughter as she meets Canio's glance.)

CANIO *(terribile)*
Ah! Tu mi sfidi! E ancor non l'hai capita
Ch'io non ti cedo? Il nome, o la tua vita! Il
nome!

CANIO *(wild with rage)*
Ah! You defy me still! And still don't
understand that I'll not yield? His name or
your life! His name!

NEDDA
Ah! No, per mia madre!
indegna esser poss'io,
Quello che vuoi, ma vil non son, per Dio!

NEDDA
Ah! No, by my mother! I may be unworthy, all you will, but, by God, I am no
coward!

BEPPE
Bisogna uscire, Tonio!

BEPPE
We must go!

TONIO
Taci, sciocco!

TONIO
Silence, fool!

NEDDA
Di quel tuo sdegno è l'amor mio più forte.
Non parlerò. No, a costo della morte!

NEDDA
My love is stronger than your raging!
I will not speak! Not if it cost my life!

(a murmur in the crowd)

CANIO *(urlando afferra un coltello)*
Il nome! Il nome!

CANIO *(shrieking as he seizes a knife)*
His name! His name!

NEDDA
No!

NEDDA
No!

SILVIO (*snudando il pugnale*)
Santo diavolo!
Fa davvero...

SILVIO (*drawing a dagger*)
By the devil,
he means it...

(*Convulsed with rage, Canio seizes Nedda and stabs her with the knife.*)

BEPPE E LA FOLLA
Che fai?!

BEPPE AND THE CROWD
What are you doing?

CANIO
A te!

CANIO
This for you!

NEDDA
Ah!

NEDDA
Ah!

CANIO
A te!

CANIO
And this!

BEPPE E LA FOLLA
Ferma!

BEPPE AND THE CROWD
Stop!

CANIO
Di morte negli spasimi
Lo dirai!

CANIO
In your death spasm
you'll tell me!

NEDDA
Soccorso...Silvio!

NEDDA
Help!...Silvio!

SILVIO (*arrivando in scena*)
Nedda!

SILVIO (*rushing onto the inner stage*)
Nedda!

CANIO

CANIO

(*turns like a beast, leaps on Silvio and stabs him.*)

Ah! Sei tu! Ben venga!

Ah, then! It's you! Welcome!

(Silvio collapses to the floor.)

LA FOLLA
Gesummaria!

THE CROWD
Jesus and Mary!

(Several of the men rush to disarm Canio. Stupefied and motionless, he lets his knife slip to the floor.)

CANIO
La commedia è finita!

CANIO
The comedy is ended!

FINE

END

English translation of Pagliacci © EMI
(U.S.) Ltd., 1954

Cavalleria Rusticana

PIETRO MASCAGNI

COMPACT DISC ONE   70:23:00

I Pagliacci

RUGGIERO LEONCAVALLO

COMPACT DISC TWO   73:20:00

Atto Primo/Act One
SCENA PRIMO/SCENE ONE